900 YEARS OF
ENGLISH COSTUME

From the Eleventh to the Twentieth Century

Written and Illustrated by
NANCY BRADFIELD A.R.C.A.

PEERAGE BOOKS

First published in Great Britain in 1938 by
George G. Harrap & Co Ltd under the title
English Historical Costumes

This edition published in 1987 by
Peerage Books
59 Grosvenor Street
London W1

This edition (revised, enlarged, reset,
with additional illustrations) © Nancy Sayer 1970

ISBN 1 85052 054 2

Printed in Czechoslovakia

50644

INTRODUCTION

MUCH of what has happened in the past that has been of value or importance has been the result of man's efforts; therefore to understand and appreciate people or communities it is extremely helpful to know what they looked like and how they were clothed.

I have attempted here only to draw attention to the main styles of dress that have been worn in England from the time when the earliest visual records were made and to give approximately the periods when the main changes in fashion occurred.

Usually the shape or the cut of the garment is largely determined by the material available at the time. The soft draping of the medieval woollen dress contrasts greatly with the rich brocades, velvets, and embroidered garments that were padded out or displayed over the farthingales of the sixteenth century. Likewise the elaborate stiff silks of the first half of the eighteenth century, which were distended over the hooped petticoat, gave way to the thinner silks and printed cottons of the looped-up draperies of the polonaise in the latter part of the century, which were in turn followed by the thin and filmy muslins that floated round the idealized classic form of the early nineteenth century.

Dress styles have changed through the centuries, in the same way as the manner of speaking has changed and the way in which men and women move about. For example, the walk of a medieval woman and the way she sat were quite different from the way in which a Victorian would have walked or sat in her crinoline dress, or an Edwardian matron in her straight-fronted corset and trailing gown, or, yet again, a sixties' girl in her trouser suit or mini skirt.

In the earlier centuries a great gulf existed between the nobility and the peasants, the latter wearing a homespun, fairly practical form of dress, while the nobility on occasions were arrayed in fabulously rich attire. A glimpse of this is given in the Paston Letters, when William Makefyrr writes to Darcy and Alyngton in January 1504, describing the meeting between Henry VII and Philip, King of Castile, at Windsor; he says, "My Lord Harry of Stafforth rod in a gown of cloth of tuyssew, tukkyd, furryd with sabulles, a hatt of goldsmyth worke and full of stons, dyamondes and rubys, rydyng upon a sorellyd courser, bardyd with a bayrd of goldsmythes wark with rosys and draguns red." And, "My Lord Markas [Thomas Grey, Marquis of Dorset] . . . with a cott apon hys bak, the body of goldsmyths wark, the slevys of cremysyne velvyt, with letters of gold."

In social and financial position the Pastons were well above the level of the peasants, but this is what John Paston junior wrote to his father in November 1462: "The berer herof schuld bye me a gowne with pert of the money . . . for I have but on gowne at Framyngham and an other here, and that is my levere[1] gowne, and we must were hem every day for the mor part, and one gowne without change wyll sone be done."

In September 1465 he wrote this time to his mother, Margaret Paston, who was in London, "that I myth have sent me home by the same messenger ii peyir hose, i peyir blak and an othyr payir roset, whyche be redy made for me at the hosers with the crokyd bak, next to the Blak Freyrs Gate within Ludgate . . . and [if] the blak hose be payid for he wyll send me the roset un payd for. I beseche yow that this ger be not forgot, for I have not an hole hose for to doon; I trowe they schall cost both payir viii s." One of the fascinating things here is that the word "ger" (gear) is still used today by the teenager when referring to clothes.

Many things contribute to changes in fashion: inventions of new machines and materials, trade and the exchange of ideas with foreign countries, social prestige, and improvement in transport and living conditions, to mention only a few. Changes sometimes were slow, at other times rapid, but as the centuries have progressed they appear to have occurred with ever-increasing frequency.

In the past an item perhaps was only hinted at, and a number of years then passed by before it caught the fancy and became fashionable or commonplace. In the 1770's powdered hair and wigs were the height of fashion, but in fact "white hair" was being tried out by some young women a hundred years earlier than this. On May 11th, 1667, Pepys wrote in his Diary: "My wife being dressed this day in fair hair did make me so mad, that I spoke not one word with her, though I was ready to burst with anger . . . on my way home discovered my trouble to my wife for her white locks . . . I would not endure it." On the following day "comes my wife to me in her nightgown . . . would promise to wear white locks no more in my sight". Occasionally a new fashion has been launched which was an immediate success. A month after the Great Fire of London Pepys again supplies us with interesting information: "Oct. 8th, 1666. . . . The King hath yesterday in Council, declared his resolution of setting a fashion for clothes, which he will never alter." "Oct. 15th, 1666. This day the King begins to put on his vest, . . . being a long cassocke close to the body, of black cloth and pinked with white silk under it, and a coat over it . . . and upon the whole I wish the King may keep it, for it is a very fine and handsome garment." This, in fact, was the forerunner of the modern man's coat and waistcoat, or 'vest', and it marked the end of the doublet.

By the nineteenth century new fashions were being adopted much more quickly, not only from town to country people, but on the social scale as well. A letter written to *The Lady's Monthly Museum*, October 1801, makes this very plain: "What is become of the race of plain-dressing, docile and obedient beings who formerly served as cooks or housemaids, or maids of all work, in a family? . . . During a late excursion to Brighton, I enquired, as I passed through the weald of Sussex, when, to my astonishment, I found nothing but *young ladies, delicately arrayed in white*, with their heads *à la Brutus*, who declared they were all anxious for places and wished to go out to service. One of them informed me that she had

[1] *Livery, such as would have been worn by an apprentice to a City Company.*

6

lately left her place, and could have an excellent character; her only reason for quitting being that her mistress would not suffer her to drink tea twice a day, and could not abide her wearing feathers in her hat on a Sunday."

Some of the finest surviving figures showing the dress of past centuries are to be found on the tombs in many of our churches, abbeys, and cathedrals, but a number of superb effigies and monumental brasses are hidden away in small country churches, which because of their remote situation have been saved from damage.

Illuminated manuscripts and tapestries provide another valuable source for study, and, together with paintings and engravings, they have recorded the shape or colour of garments long since rotted away to dust.

Rare examples of sixteenth- and seventeenth-century clothes have survived, along with many from the eighteenth century onwards, and a number of museums have invaluable collections on display. Prints, fashion plates, and photographs can help to complete the picture, although some of these at times show an idealized version of dress, rather than what was actually worn.

The main part of my studies was at first centred in the costume galleries of the London Museum, and the Victoria and Albert Museum and the Print Room there; it was at that time that James Laver first put forward the idea of having my work published, and I wish to express my most sincere thanks to him for his help and interest, which ultimately made this idea materialize.

I owe thanks to many others who have since aided me in my research, and to firms who have been so helpful in reply to my queries, especially I. and R. Morley. Ltd, and their "friendly competitors", also British Nylon Spinners, Ltd, Lightning Fasteners, Ltd, Newey and Tayler, Ltd, Georges The Hosiery Specialists, Ltd, and P. F. J. Skinner (Footwear).

My thanks too to Birmingham Public Libraries and the Gloucestershire College of Art Library, and a special word of thanks to the Reference Department of Cheltenham Public Library and to the Costume and Textile Department of the Victoria and Albert Museum for help since my student days.

Finally, I wish to thank most warmly the photographers, the museums and galleries, and all those who have so wholeheartedly given me their co-operation in assembling the material for this third edition.

NANCY BRADFIELD

PLATES
showing some sources for study

Plate I—

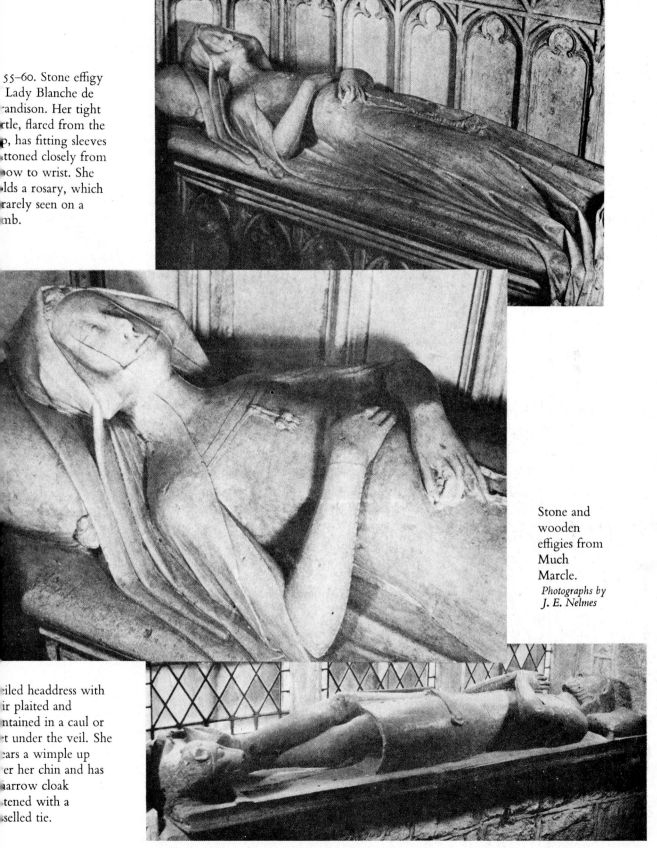

55–60. Stone effigy
Lady Blanche de
randison. Her tight
rtle, flared from the
p, has fitting sleeves
ttoned closely from
ow to wrist. She
lds a rosary, which
rarely seen on a
mb.

Stone and
wooden
effigies from
Much
Marcle.
*Photographs by
J. E. Nelmes*

iled headdress with
ir plaited and
ntained in a caul or
t under the veil. She
ars a wimple up
er her chin and has
arrow cloak
tened with a
selled tie.

Mid-fourteenth-century wooden effigy, his cote-hardie buttoned at front and on sleeves.
He wears a hip belt with a dagger and purse on right side, and has pointed shoes.

c. 1340. Peasants in tunics, wearing hoods and gloves.
Below: A spinster, her head veiled, has a kirtle under side-less surcoat and an embroidered apron.

c. 1425. Tapestry, the deer hunt, the ladies have heart-shaped headdresses and long, richly patterned gowns; the men wear chaperons and the short, pleated houppelande.

Plate III—

1485. Monumental brass rubbing, she has a
butterfly headdress, jewelled collar, and a
fur-trimmed gown. *Storey-Moore Photographics*

ELIZABETH · REGINA · REGIS
EDVARDI · ANGLIE

c. 1465. Elizabeth Woodville, a rare early
painting, showing the thin gauze veil over
the decorated cap of the butterfly headdress,
and the rich fabric of collar and cuffs.
Ashmolean Museum, Oxford

c. 1405. Stone effigy; her houppelande has the
typical high neck, closely gathered folds, and
long, hanging sleeves.

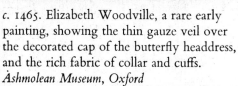

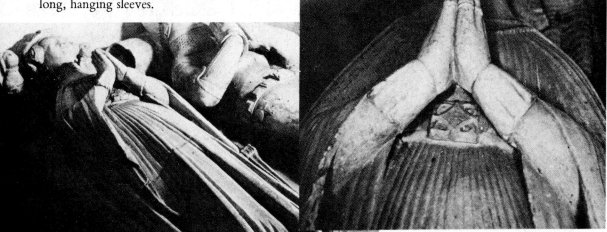

Photographs by J. E. Nelmes

Plate IV —

c. 1580. Queen Elizabeth in a fine, lace-edged ruff; her gauze veil and bodice are jewelled and embroidered, with the sleeves in black-work. She has a feather fan.

Painting at Hampton Court Palace Copyright reserved

1602. Sir Walter Raleigh and his son; both have doublets with wings; he wears trunk-hose and canions. *National Portrait Gallery*

c. 1572. Engraving of London citizens, the older man in a fur-lined gown and the lady in a Spanish farthingale.

London Museum

1616

1623. Long, flowing hair, denoting virginity, worn by Amy Seymour, who has her ring secured by a black cord. Her bodice is embroidered in silks and gold thread. *Cheltenham Museum and Art Gallery*

Plate V

Photograph by J. E. Nelmes

c. 1643. Hester, the wife, wears a lace-edged whisk and skirted bodice, favoured since c. 1630. *Ashmolean Museum, Oxford*

1682. King Charles II wearing a periwig, long coat, and cravat; his Queen in an open robe and petticoat. *London Museum*

6. The daughter, in high hair style [and] wheel farthingale, has a bodice [sim]ilar to the son's doublet.

Photographs by J. E. Nelmes

Plate VI—

1755–60. Sack-backed gown, flounced and furbelowed.

*Cheltenham
Museum and
Art Gallery*

*Photograph by
J. E. Nelmes*

c. 1745–55. Man's coat, waistcoat, and
breeches of velvet, woven to shape.
Left: c. 1733–35. Brocaded silk, made into
a dress, style of *c.* 1755, with embroidered
muslin ruffles and green silk quilted
petticoat, *c.* 1740.

THE AFFECTIONATE SISTERS.

1788. Men in wigs and women in huge
hats and puffed neckerchiefs.

Photograph by J. E. Nelmes

*Victoria and
Albert
Museum.
Crown
copyright*

Plate VII—

*Both fashion plates below
photographed by J. E. Nelmes*

c. 1860. Full-skirted dress over crinoline frame with bolero and bishop sleeves; the man has a double-breasted frock-coat, worn, as was usual, with lighter trousers.
Photographs from family album, enlarged by J. E. Nelmes

1799. Trained winter day dresses of silk and muslin, with turbans.

1876. Walking costumes with trains and tied-back, low bustles.

c. 1883. Mauve corded silk day dress, with bustle rising to new position of the eighties.
City of Birmingham copyright

Plate VIII—

*The Museum
of Costume, Bath*

*Photograph by
West Advertising, Ltd.*

1900-6.
Edwardian
women in lo[ng]
trailing gown[s]
with large ha[ts]
and parasols.
The centre fig[ure]
and front view
left shows a
dove-grey co[at]
with embroid[ery]
in silk thread
made by Wo[rth]
for Lady Cur[zon]

Darby Photographic Service

1907. Visiting gown in
mulberry velvet, with
long, voluminous skirts.

C 61.   25/9

1916. Advertisement for a jumper frock, the dresses
now, for the first time, being short to above the
ankle. *Photographs by J. E. Nelmes*

1967-68. Jackie, in leather tunic and mini
skirt and popular long-hair style; Barry, in
polo-neck sweater, jacket, and slim, parallel-line
trousers. *Storey-Moore Photographics*

CONTENTS

NOTE

The use of italics in the marginal headings denotes that the particular feature thus indicated is introduced for the first time.

William 1 (1066-87)

Norman

Saxon

1   2   3   4   5

1

WILLIAM I (1066–87)

Men's Fashions

THE most outstanding difference between the Saxons and the Normans was the manner of doing the hair; otherwise the costumes were almost identical, the Saxons having adopted many of the Norman fashions before the Conquest.

The tunic was fairly loose-fitting, and reached to the knee for ordinary wear. It was put on over the head, so the neck was moderately low, or with a slit in the front (Figs. 2, 3, 4, 5), showing the under-tunic (Fig. 2). The top was pouched over the belt (Figs. 1, 3), and the skirt was sometimes slit up at the sides (Fig. 3). At first the Normans also wore a divided skirt, or 'shorts' (Fig. 4).

The sleeves were either loose at the top and tight at the wrist (Figs. 3, 4, 5), or shorter, hanging wide from the elbow, showing the sleeve of the under-tunic (Fig. 1). Longer garments were worn for State functions (see p. 14, Fig. 2). Woollen cloths or linens were used and frequently covered with geometric patterns, stripes, etc., but the decorative borders, either embroidered or woven, were more general. Saxon women were famed for their beautiful embroidery, and it was used by them on clothes of both rich and poor, and later was used extensively by the Normans (p. 14, Figs. 2, 3).

The breeches, or 'braies', covered the limbs from the waist downward and were very like linen trousers, either with feet attached to keep them in place or with a loop under the arch of the foot. They were held up by means of a cord running through the hem at the waist. The upper classes wore more fitting breeches, often having plain or crossed bands from the knee to the ankle (Figs. 1, 2, 4). Only the lower classes wore loose leg-coverings.

Coarse stockings, or hose, made of more loosely woven material, were sometimes pulled over the breeches, covering the feet and legs up to the knee (Fig. 3). Both the breeches and hose were brightly coloured; they were of cloth cut on the cross.

The shoes were high, fitting round the ankle. They were made of leather.

Semicircular and square-shaped cloaks were fastened by brooch or cord (Fig. 1, and p. 18, Fig. 6) and made of thicker cloth than the tunic.

A hood, or cowl, was worn with the cloak in bad weather (Fig. 1).

Though the Saxons still wore their hair long and had their faces bearded, the Norman fashion of cropping the hair, almost as it is today, with the face clean-shaven, was much more usual (Figs. 2, 3, 4). During the first few years the back of the head was so closely shaven that it looked almost bald, but later the hair was grown longer.

Light blue, red, and green were fashionable; the colours of the coarse homespun woollen cloth called 'russet' were red-brown and grey; yellow was also worn, and black—a colour which had been used a great deal by the Danes.

Marginal notes: Tunic · Under-tunic, or shirt · Sleeves · Embroidery · Breeches · Hose · Shoes · Cloaks · Hood · Hair · Colours

William II (1087-1100)

1   2   3   4

2

WILLIAM II (1087–1100)

Men's Fashions

TUNICS were long and lavishly decorated. Flowing hair and beards returned to favour.

The under-tunic with the fitting sleeves was longer during this reign (Fig. 1). **Under-tunic**

The long, richly embroidered tunics of the Normans and Flemings who came to **Tunic** the English court in great numbers were soon adopted by the fashionably minded men. The skirts, reaching to the ankles, were sometimes slit at the sides (Fig. 2), and for full dress the gowns were so long that they trailed on the ground. The tunic was pouched at the waist, almost hiding the girdle (Figs. 1, 2). By 1100 the sleeves **Sleeves** became very wide and long, and were turned back in a deep cuff showing the lining (Fig. 2). The middle and lower classes still wore the short tunic with moderate sleeves (Fig. 4). Woollen cloths and linens were used as before.

The breeches remained the same (Figs. 2, 4), but those worn by the nobles were **Breeches** much more fitting.

The short type of stocking was still in use, though seldom seen under the long **Hose** tunics.

The shoes of the nobles were slightly more exaggerated in cut, otherwise there **Shoes** was no change.

Cloaks were longer and fuller. The short cloak was retained by the middle and **Cloaks** lower classes (Fig. 4). The pallium, or cloak, adopted from the East, was draped round *Pallium* the hips and over the shoulder (Fig. 3). Fur-lined cloaks were quite common among the nobility.

Men usually left their heads uncovered, but the hood (see p. 12), and the small *Hats* beret, or Phrygian cap, was used when the weather was bad (Fig. 4, and p. 22, Fig. 3).

Short hair went out of fashion; it was now cut in quite a long 'bob' covering the **Hair** ears. Beards were seen again and were very fashionable before the end of the century. Bands were sometimes worn round the head (Fig. 3).

Swords and daggers were not worn with civil dress throughout the Middle Ages, **Swords** though the dagger was sometimes seen during the fourteenth century.

Colours of the materials are on p. 13. **Colours**

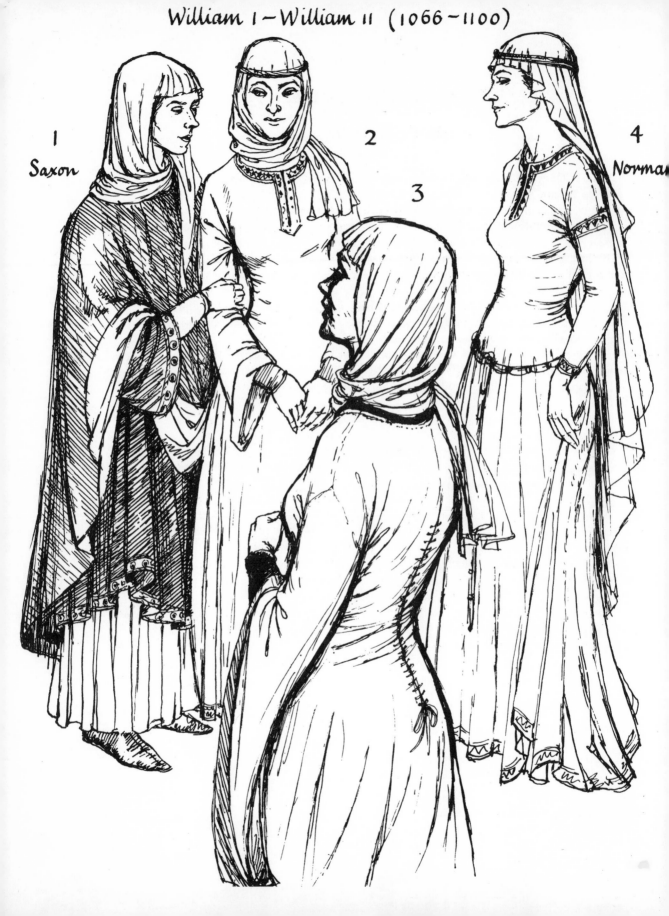

William I - William II (1066-1100)

1
Saxon

2

3

4
Norman

3

WILLIAM I—WILLIAM II (1066–1100)

Women's Fashions

THE only appreciable difference between the Saxon and the Norman women was that the gown of the latter was made tight from shoulder to hip.

The sleeves were generally the only part of the under-tunic that were visible (Figs. 2, 3), except when the short over-dress was worn, then the skirt was also seen (Fig. 1). *Under-tunic, or smock*

The fitting gown became popular (Figs. 2, 4); the upper part was tightly laced at the back (Fig. 3), and although the skirt was full, hanging in heavy folds from the hips, it was not joined separately to the bodice. The short, looser gown was still used by some of the middle and lower classes (Fig. 1). The neck was round and slit down the front (Figs. 2, 4), and the sleeves were either tight down to the wrist (Fig. 4) or shorter and fairly wide from the elbow (Figs. 1, 2). By the end of the century these became even wider and hung almost to the knees (Fig. 3). Long girdles were sometimes worn round the hips (Fig. 4). Wool and linen cloths were used, also russet (a coarse, homespun woollen cloth of red-brown or grey colour). The borders of women's dresses were also elaborately embroidered. *Gown, or kirtle* *Sleeves* *Russet*

Long semicircular or square-shaped cloaks, fastened with a cord, were usual, and the rounded type with a centre-opening for the head was occasionally seen (Fig. 1). Cloaks

Women wore short hose, gartered at the knee. Hose

The shoes were similar to the men's, but were seldom seen owing to the length of the gown. Shoes

The hair, long and sometimes plaited, was hidden under the veil during this period. Hair

The fine linen veil covering the head hung loose at the back, or was draped round the shoulders, and was sometimes kept in place by a narrow band or circlet. Veils

Light blue, red, and greens were fashionable; black, yellow, red-browns, and grey were also worn. Colours

Henry I – Stephen (1100–54)

1
1100–35

2
1130

3

4

middle-class

5

6

4

HENRY I—STEPHEN (1100-54)

Men's Fashions

LONG hair and extravagant gowns remained in fashion.

 The under-tunic was still worn, but the length varied (Fig. 2).   *Under-tunic*

 The long tunic of the preceding reign was fashionable until the middle of   *Tunic* the century. The neck and hem continued to be elaborately embroidered, and sometimes the chest and upper arm was also decorated with an embroidered band, as in Fig. 3. The full skirt was frequently caught up on either side in the front (Fig. 1), or pulled through the girdle (Fig. 2). The neck was cut low (Fig. 2), and both wide and narrow sleeves were worn (Figs. 1, 2, 3). Middle classes wore the short tunic, either   *Sleeves* hanging loose or girdled at the waist (Figs. 3, 4). Cloth was of wool or linen.

 The breeches were not altered until 1150, being long from the waist down to the   *Breeches* feet (Fig. 4), but after that date, when a longer type of hose came into fashion, they reached to the knee only, and henceforward were hidden under the tunic.

 From 1150 the hose were made long, fitting the leg well, to above the knee;   *Hose* the tops were wide with the breeches tucked into them. The front of this stocking was pointed, with a tape attached, and this tape was tied round the girdle running through the hem of the breeches at the waist. (The girdle was exposed at the required places in front to make this possible. See p. 22, Fig. 5.)

 Shoes were made in quite a variety of shapes, some like small boots, others cut   *Shoes* away in the front, but all had pointed toes (Fig. 5). There is little evidence to be found in the art of this period of the reputed curled toes supposed to have been fashionable (Fig. 1).

 Wraps and cloaks were as before and fastened with buckles or cords (Fig. 6).   *Cloaks*

 The cowl, or hood, generally had a point at the back, and the cape part covering the   *Hood* shoulders was called the gorget (Fig. 4). This hood was worn by the lower classes   *Gorget* for over three hundred years (Plate II).

 The hair was long, occasionally reaching to the shoulders (Figs. 1, 3), and the   *Hair* fashionable men brushed it forward in a fringe over the forehead.

 Colours are on p. 17; no new ones are mentioned.   *Colours*

Henry I – Stephen
(1100 – 54)

1

nobility

1125–75

1100–35

2

3

4

undergarment

HENRY I—STEPHEN (1100–54)

Women's Fashions

LONG hair and long sleeves were the most outstanding features of women's fashions.

The undergarment was made of fine linen and had a pleated appearance. This effect was probably obtained by wringing it, when wet, from neck to hem into one long twist, and leaving it so until dry. The sleeves were long, following the fashion (Figs. 1, 4); they were made separately and gathered in to the armholes. — Undergarment, or smock

The gown itself remained as before (Fig. 2), but the fashionable sleeves were extremely wide from below the elbow, often reaching to the ground (Fig. 1). When this was exaggerated, as most fashions are sooner or later, they were knotted up out of the way. Gowns appeared to be made of finer cloths or linens during these two reigns, as the draperies in the paintings and effigies of this period were noticeably more delicate than the heavy folds generally seen. — Gown / Sleeves

Between 1125 and 1175 ladies of high rank wore special long girdles for State functions (Fig. 1). They were high round the waist in front, crossed at the back, and brought forward low on the hips, where the silken ends attached to this flat belt were tied together and hung down the front, nearly to the hem of the gown. — *Girdle*

Full cloaks were worn as before (Fig. 1), also a new garment called the pelisse (Fig. 3), of Eastern origin, which was only worn by the noblewomen who could afford such luxuries. — Cloaks / *Pelisse*

Until 1120 the hair was concealed under the veil; thereafter the two plaits bound round with silk or ribbons hung to the knee, or lower (Figs. 1, 3); sometimes false hair was used to add to their length. Young girls wore their hair loose (Fig. 2). — Hair / *False hair*

Upper classes retained the veil, now very long, for out of doors until 1150. The band worn round the head (Figs. 1, 3) was of silk, or gold set with precious stones for the lady of rank. — Veil

Colours remained as before, no fresh ones being mentioned (p. 17). — Colours

Henry II - Richard I (1154-99)

1189-99

1

2

3

4

5

6

5

HENRY II—RICHARD I (1154–99)

Men's Fashions

A DIFFERENT type of tunic made its appearance before 1190.

New and expensive materials were worn by noblemen.

Both the long and the short tunic of the first half of the century were **Tunic** still worn (Figs. 1, 2). At the end of Henry II's reign a new type appeared and remained in fashion until 1300. The sleeves were the most striking feature; they were **Sleeves** wide and loose from the waist, but narrowed down to a small cuff (Figs. 3, 4). The skirts were long to the ankle, and were generally cut up the front. The girdle became more ornate and had one long hanging end (Fig. 4).

Royalty and noblemen wore a new expensive worsted cloth of scarlet wool and *Scarlet cloth* a fine soft woollen cloth. Otherwise coarser woollen cloths, russets, and linens were general.

The hose remained the same as in the previous reign, fitting the leg to above the **Hose** knee and fastened to the girdle of the breeches (Fig. 5). Coloured or gilded crossbands of leather were sometimes worn right up the leg by the rich (Fig. 3). Poorer men or travellers occasionally wore them to the knee only (Fig. 1). Long hose with leather soles were worn without shoes (Fig. 3).

Ankle-fitting shoes were retained by the poorer people (Figs. 1, 2). The new **Shoes** low-cut shoe was more usual for the wealthy (Fig. 4). Boots reaching to the calf were quite popular during this century; the tops were turned over showing the coloured lining (Fig. 6).

Cloaks were full and fastened with brooch or cord (Figs. 3, 4); also cloaks of skins **Cloaks** with hoods attached were used by travellers at the end of this period (Fig. 1).

Hats with a high crown and turned-up brim were sometimes worn over the hood **Hoods, hats** (Fig. 2). The flat, wide-brimmed hat was occasionally seen on travellers (Fig. 1). Varieties of the small cap-shape, or beret, some of the Phrygian shape, were used by the upper classes (Figs. 3, 4).

The hair was cut shorter but still 'bobbed'. Small pointed beards were fashionable **Hair** for a short while at the end of Richard I's reign. **Gloves and**

Gloves were worn (Figs. 3, 4). A pouch or money purse hung from the girdle (Fig. 2). *purse*

Colours are shown on the women's page (p. 25). **Colours**

Henry II – Richard I (1154-99)

1190

1

2

1189-99

3

115

5

1170

HENRY II—RICHARD I (1154–99)

Women's Fashions

THE long plaits of hair began to go out of fashion by the end of the century. The throat was occasionally covered by the wimple.

The long, tight sleeves were the only part of the under-tunic that was **Under-tunic** visible (Figs. 1, 2, 3, 4) except when a short type of gown was worn, then the long, full skirt could be seen (Fig. 1).

The graceful fitting gown, often laced down the back, was little changed, the **Gown** skirt hung in heavy folds to the ground (Figs. 2, 4). The short form of Saxon tunic was still sometimes seen (Fig. 1). The lower rounded neck (Figs. 2, 4) did not have the slit down the front (Fig. 3). The very wide sleeves (Figs. 2, 4), though worn until **Sleeves** the reign of John (p. 28), gradually became less popular. The new scarlet cloth and the **Scarlet cloth** fine, soft woollen cloths were used by noblewomen and often beautifully embroidered; gowns were also of coarser woollen cloths, russet, and linens.

Cloaks were quite general (Fig. 1), and made of the heavier materials. **Cloaks**

The long plaits of hair (Fig. 4) were sometimes coiled round the head (Figs. 2, 5), **Hair** or on either side over the ears (Fig. 3).

The short linen veils with the gold or silken band round the head came into fashion **Veils** again in the reign of Richard I (Figs. 1, 3).

In 1170 the barbette was introduced (Fig. 5), being a linen band passing under the *Barbette* chin and over the head. In 1190 a linen covering for the throat, called the wimple, *Wimple* appeared (Fig. 1). It was tucked into the dress and often veiled the chin. It was pinned to the hair above the ears (p. 32, Fig. 1), or on top of the head under the veil.

Women's stockings were gartered at the knee. **Hose**

There was very little difference between men's and women's shoes. **Shoes**

Scarlet—the colour of the new material—was worn by noblemen and noble women. **Colours** Green and watchet (a light greenish blue) were fashionable, and yellow, red, tawny (a yellow-brown), red-browns, black, and greys were worn.

John – Henry III (1199-1272)

1   1199-1216

2

3   1247

4   1230

5   farm-worker

1250

6

JOHN—HENRY III (1199–1272)

Men's Fashions

TWO new types of supertunic were worn in Henry III's reign.
 The tunic with the wide-shaped sleeves and long skirt slit up the front remained unchanged. Youths of the middle and lower classes still wore the shorter tunic that reached to above the knee.

Tunic

The hem of the tunic, and perhaps the shoulder cape, was sometimes cut up into deep scallops (Figs. 1, 2); this 'dagging' was later used a great deal from *c.* 1346.

Dagging

After 1200 a supertunic was made from one long strip of material (Fig. 4). The sides could be left open or sewn together up to the hips; it generally reached to the calf and was sometimes split up the front. The long girdle was worn over this garment.

Supertunics

In 1225 another type occurred which hung free from the shoulders to the ankle or calf (Fig. 3), and was worn until 1300, and it often had a hood attached. The sleeves were unusual, being very wide and long, and gathered into small pleats on the shoulder. There was a short slit in the front so that the arm could pass through, leaving the sleeve hanging loose to the knee. A long sleeve, similar to this, but without the shoulder pleats, was still being worn in 1525.

Sleeves

Both tunic and supertunics were made of the same materials as before (p. 23), also a woollen cloth of yellow-brown colour; canvas was known during this period. Fur-lined supertunics called 'pelissons' were not uncommon.

Canvas
Pelissons

The leg-coverings remained the same, but cross-bands were rare after 1200 (Fig. 1).

Hose

The toes of the shoes and boots were slightly more pointed.

Shoes

The cloak, replaced by the supertunic, was now used only on State occasions or for travelling (Fig. 2).

Cloaks

The hood still remained the principal head-covering; the cape part was often worn separately (Fig. 2).

Hoods

Small round hats were more common (Figs. 1, 2), and sometimes put on over a white linen undercap, or coif, that covered the hair and was tied under the chin (Fig. 5), and was worn by peasants and men of wealth alike, but well before the sixteenth century it was confined to the learned professions or aged, when it was often of black cloth.

Hats
Coif

The 'bobbed' hair remained fashionable, beards disappearing until about 1350.

Hair

Colours of materials are on p. 29.

Colours

John - Henry III (1199-1272)

1

2

3

4

5

1216-72

1216 -72

1199 -1216

JOHN—HENRY III (1199–1272)

Women's Fashions

THE hair was concealed again by 1216, and the wide, exaggerated sleeves were replaced by closer-fitting ones.

The under-tunic was seldom visible and remained as before. — **Under-tunic**

The gown, still long and full, had a fairly low round neck (Fig. 3), which was — **Gown**
sometimes open down the front and fastened with a brooch (Fig. 5). The long girdle that was fashionable for men was also worn by the women.

The wide type of sleeve was still fairly common (Figs. 3, 4), but early in the reign — **Sleeve**
of Henry III it lost favour and small, fitting sleeves came into their own until the end of the fourteenth century, being wide under the armpit, like a man's sleeve (Figs. 2, 5).

The expensive cloth of scarlet and soft, fine woollen cloths were for noblewomen's gowns; also coarser woollen cloths, a yellow-brown cloth, russet (the red-brown or grey homespun), and linens were used.

A type of supertunic, similar to those worn by the men (p. 27), was sometimes — **Supertunic**
seen among the lower classes (Fig. 2). The long skirt was often tucked into the side opening when working, and the bottom of the gown was pinned up, showing the underskirts. Aprons were worn by middle-class and poorer women (Fig. 5, p. 40). — *Aprons*

The full cloaks were richly lined and embroidered (Figs. 4, 5). Fur was often used — **Cloaks**
for the lining.

The long plaits were sometimes seen during the first year or two (Fig. 3), but the — **Hair**
hair was generally arranged in large coils on either side of the head (Figs. 1, 2, 5); this fashion became very popular.

The hair was usually covered with a short veil (Fig. 4) or small linen cap-shapes — **Veils, etc.**
(Figs. 1, 2). By 1220 the narrow band, or circlet, hitherto worn round the head, was — *Fillet*
widened out into a stiff band or fillet of linen, with the top wider than the bottom (Figs. 1, 5). It was worn with the barbette—the linen band that was wound round the head and under the chin (see p. 24, Fig. 5).

Purses drawn together with cords at the top hung from the girdle (Fig. 5); they — **Purse**
were easily cut away by thieves; hence the term 'cutpurse' used in medieval times.

Small round hats were occasionally worn by women when travelling (Fig. 4). — **Hats**

Scarlet and purple for nobles, green, watchet (light greenish blue), and murrey — **Colours**
(deep purple-red) were very fashionable among all classes; red, tawny, red-browns, and greys were still worn.

Edward 1 (1272-1307)

1

2

3

1290

4

5

7

EDWARD I (1272–1307)

Men's Fashions

VELVET was first mentioned in 1303, and was used in churches or worn by royalty, a less expensive material called fustian that looked very like velvet being worn by nobles from 1300. Serge was also mentioned in 1303.

The long tunic, introduced in 1189 (p. 23), was very much the same (Fig. 1), sleeves and skirt only being visible. The sleeves fitted more to the arm, and the skirt, sometimes slit up the front, hung to just above the ankle; it was girdled at the waist. | Tunic

The supertunic of 1225 was unchanged (Figs. 1, 2). It hung loose from the shoulder to below the calf; the front, and sometimes the sides as well, was open up to the hips. The very full sleeves pleated on the shoulder were unaltered (Fig. 1), though a plainer, loose-fitting sleeve became fairly common (Figs. 2, 3). The hood was worn as before with this supertunic sometimes sewn on, or there was a plain, upright collar round the neck (Fig. 2). Fur linings were general. | Supertunic — Sleeves

The expensive cloth of scarlet and the new velvety material (fustian) were worn by nobles for tunic and supertunic (velvet, as previously mentioned, was for royalty only), also fine woollen cloths, coarser cloths, and russets were otherwise used, and serge for the outer garments. | *Fustian* *Velvet* — *Serge*

The leg-coverings were the same, still being well-fitting to above the knee, and fastened to the girdle of the breeches. | Hose

The pointed shoes were often fur-lined (Fig. 5) and decorated with a coloured or embroidered band at the instep among the upper classes. | Shoes

Large cloaks of serge or thick woollen cloths were still used in bad weather. | Cloaks

Though men often went bareheaded until nearly the end of the fourteenth century, hoods were the most usual head-covering. The point at the back of the cowl developed into a long tail called a lirapipe (Fig. 3), which was sometimes wound round the head (Fig. 4). | Hoods — *Lirapipe*

The small cap-shape, or beret, with the tiny point on top and the rolled brim was also worn (Fig. 1), and the wide-brimmed hat for travellers (p. 22, Fig. 1). | Hats

'Bobbed' hair was still fashionable. | Hair

Buckles, etc., were gradually replaced by buttons (Figs. 1, 2); these had been used since the twelfth century, chiefly at first for ornament. | *Buttons*

Gloves were worn by noblemen or high officials. | Gloves

Colours are shown on p. 33. | Colours

31

Edward 1 (1272 - 1307)

1300
1

2

3

4

5

6

EDWARD I (1272–1307)

Women's Fashions

A WIDER form of hairdressing became fashionable, and a new coarse net or wire covering, called the caul or fret, was worn over the hair.

The long under-tunic with the fitting sleeves was unaltered (Figs. 1, 2). *Under-tunic*

The gown was tight to the hips as before, and the skirt was full and very long, the *Gown* fullness being obtained by inserting gores; the neck tended to be cut lower.

The sleeves were sometimes shorter, hanging wide from below the elbow, other- *Sleeves* wise the tight-fitting sleeves remained unaltered. The borders of the gown were often beautifully embroidered (Fig. 2).

The fine scarlet cloth, fustian (silky-looking like velvet), and fine woollen materials *Fustian* were used for the noblewomen's gowns; woollen cloths, russet, linens, and canvas, were otherwise used.

Velvet was for royalty only. *Velvet*

Cloaks were very full and made of serge or thick woollen cloths, lined with softer *Cloaks* materials (Fig. 2).

The fashion of coiling the hair over either ear was adopted by rich and poor. *Hair* Young girls still had their hair loose with a silken band round the head.

The hair was now covered with a coarse net, a caul or fret, which was made of *Caul,* silk or even gold (Figs. 3, 4). In its later richly decorative state it persisted for nearly *or fret* two hundred years.

The wimple (p. 24, Fig. 1) was generally worn throughout this reign (Figs. 1, 2), *Wimple* and also the veil. Widows had the wimple pleated in front and covering the chin *Widow's* (Fig. 6). The plain wimple also was sometimes worn over the chin (Plate I). *weeds*

In 1290 the linen fillet round the head, that was worn with the barbette (p. 28, *Headdress* Fig. 5), spread out sideways over the wider form of hairdressing (Fig. 3). The top edge of this band was sometimes pleated on to a flat piece of stiffened linen covering the crown of the head (Fig. 5).

The shoes had pointed toes and were cut similar to the male shoe. They were rarely *Shoes* seen under those long, full-skirted gowns.

Scarlet for the nobility, also murrey (deep purple-red), green, watchet (light *Colours* greenish blue), light blue, slate colour, tawny, brown, red, reddish browns, and greys were worn.

33

Edward II (1307-27)

1   2   3   4

1320

5

6

a   b   c

8

EDWARD II (1307–27)

Men's Fashions

THE hood was occasionally used as a hat; more new materials were mentioned during this reign.

The sleeves of the tunic were more fitting (Fig. 1)—the tunic is here partly hidden by the supertunic), otherwise this garment was no different from those worn in the preceding reign. The short tunic (Fig. 2) was still worn by youths, and the sleeves were sometimes left undone from wrist to elbow so that they hung loose, showing the under-sleeve. **Tunic**

The simple sleeveless supertunic of 1236 (p. 26, Fig. 4) was still to be seen (Fig. 1). In 1320 a very wide variety of this, called the garnache, was introduced (Fig. 4). The sides, as before, could be left open or sewn together up to the hips, and the shoulder-piece extended over the arm to the elbow. The oddly shaped lapels at the neck were peculiar to male garments during this century. **Supertunic** *Garnache*

Gold or silver tissue was much favoured by royalty and worn until the reign of Charles II. A soft woollen cloth of narrow width was worn by the wealthy, otherwise materials were as before (p. 31), the heavier cloths, serge, etc., being used more for the outer garments. *Gold tissue* *Kersey*

There was no alteration in leg-coverings; they were of various colours (Plate II). **Hose**

Shoes also remained the same. Note that the 'point' of this type of shoe was always in line with the big toe. **Shoes**

Large circular cloaks, sometimes with a hood sewn to the neck opening in the centre, were of serge, etc. (Fig. 3). **Cloaks**

The hood was still worn in the usual manner (Fig. 2), though it was occasionally used as a hat (Fig. 5), and later called the chaperon. The opening for the face (Fig. 6b) was put on over the head, with the edge rolled back to make a brim; thus the shoulder-cape, or gorget (Fig. 6c), hung down one side of the head, and the lirapipe (Fig. 6a) the other; or the lirapipe could be twisted round the head (Fig. 5). This did not become really fashionable until 1377. **Hoods** *Chaperon*

The linen undercap, the coif (see p. 27), was still in use (Fig. 5). **Coif**

The purse, with draw-strings at the top, hung from the girdle (Fig. 2 and p. 38, Fig. 1). **Purse**

Daggers were sometimes carried, but swords were rarely seen with civil dress during the Middle Ages. Gloves were now worn by farm workers (Plate II). **Swords** **Gloves**

Colours of materials are shown on the women's page of this reign, also at p. 33. **Colours**

Edward II (1307-27)

1

1310

2   3   1325

4

low
clas
5

EDWARD II (1307–27)

Women's Fashions

THE headdresses were wider. A new gown called the sideless surcoat was also introduced, and taffeta is mentioned.

    The long, well-fitting under-tunic with the tight sleeves seen in Figs. 1, 2, 3, 4 now formed part of the dress and was called the kirtle. *Under-tunic, or kirtle*

    In 1310 a gown called the sideless surcoat was made without sleeves, and the sides slit open down to the hips (Fig. 2), a fashion probably taken from the men's simple type of supertunic (p. 26, Fig. 4). It was fairly fitting at the top and hung down in a full long skirt. The side openings were sometimes mere slits (Fig. 2), or they were cut square-shaped (Fig. 1); later the rounded form was worn and remained fashionable (Figs. 3, 4). The neck was cut round and often very low, leaving only narrow strips over the shoulders (Fig. 1). The middle-class and poor women also wore this extra garment (Fig. 5 and Plate II) nearly a century earlier (p. 28, Fig. 2), and it continued fashionable for ninety years, and up to *c.* 1525 for State wear. *Sideless surcoat*

    Taffeta, a most expensive new material, was only worn by ladies of the highest rank. Noblewomen also wore the new soft narrow cloth of wool, also the scarlet cloth and velvety material (fustian). Gowns were also of coarser cloths, russet, and linens. *Taffeta and kersey*

    The cloaks were usually full and fastened across the front with rich cords (Fig. 3). The wearer's coat of arms was often used to decorate the cloak or gown (see p. 48, Fig. 1). *Cloaks*

    The hair was still arranged in a large coil over each ear (Figs. 1, 2, 3). *Hair*

    Linen veils were held in place by the narrow band of silk or gold (Fig. 2) or draped over the high, wide headdress (Fig. 4). The wimple (Figs. 2, 3, 4) and caul or fret (Fig. 1) continued to be fashionable. The high, rounded headdress widened out still more (Fig. 1); the linen band under the chin (the barbette) was not to be seen any more after this reign. *Veils* *Wimple* *Caul*

    Cloths of gold and silver were worn by royalty and scarlet by nobles as before, otherwise colours were as in the previous reign (p. 33). *Colours*

37

middle-class

poor

1

2

3

4 1366

5

6 1350

Edward III (1327-77)

7

8

9

9

EDWARD III (1327–77)

Men's Fashions

EDWARD III encouraged the weaving trade, and many foreign craftsmen settled in England. New materials were introduced, and there was a noticeable change in men's garments. The younger men especially, of all classes, wore them short and tight, displaying the full length of the leg.

The tunic was now called the gypon, and the supertunic the cote-hardie.

The gypon was a very well-tailored form of tunic worn over the shirt. Until about 1360 it reached to the knee; thereafter it was made increasingly shorter, until it barely covered the hips. The front was well padded. The sleeves, fitting to the wrist, are seen in Fig. 3, the rest of the garment being hidden under the cote-hardie.

Buttons, lavishly used, were both functional and decorative (Figs. 1, 3, 4, 5, and Plate I).

The cote-hardie, worn over the gypon, reached to the knee until 1360 (Fig. 3), and, like the gypon, it became very short (Figs. 4, 5). It was fastened down the front by a number of small buttons to the girdle (Fig. 3), and later to the hem (Figs. 4, 5). Poorer classes wore a short cote-hardie of moderate length (Fig. 1). At first the sleeves were cut away in front to the elbow, and hung long at the back (Fig. 3). This 'flap' was later replaced by a long streamer, usually made of white material, called the tippet (Figs. 1, 5, 6). The cuffs often extended over the hand to the knuckles (Figs. 1, 5). Elderly men wore a looser tunic (Fig. 6). The girdle was set low on the hips (Figs. 1, 3 and Plate I), and nobles wore flat metal jewelled belts (Figs. 4, 5 and Plate III).

New materials used for body-garments were satin (1350), silk (1360). flannel of a fine linen, and a many-coloured worsted material (1371), also woollen cloths, russets, a new green Flemish cloth, siskin, and grey Musterdevilliers from Normandy.

The leg-coverings were still made separately (Fig. 8). From 1350 they were longer, and fastened to the inside of the gypon by short laces or points with 'tag' ends, tied through a series of corresponding holes. Long hose with leather soles were worn without shoes (Fig. 5), also very long, pointed or piked shoes.

Richly lined semicircular cloaks were fastened with two buttons on one shoulder, and made of serge or broadcloth (thick cloth of fine wool), and lined with satin, etc.

Hoods were still the usual head-covering (Figs. 1, 4, 7, 9). The cape part, with the edges dagged, was sometimes worn separately (Fig. 5). (See p. 27 for 'dagging'.)

A new beaver hat with a very high crown was popular early in the reign (Fig. 7), otherwise small round hats were much the same as before (Figs. 1, 4). From 1350 ostrich plumes or peacock feathers were used. Hats were worn indoors until 1660.

Hair remained 'bobbed'. Small beards were fairly fashionable (Figs. 4, 5).

Colours are shown on the women's page of this reign (p. 41). Particoloured garments (Figs. 1, 5) became very fashionable for men.

Gypon,
or gipon

Sleeves

Buttons

Cote-hardie

Sleeves

Tippet

Satin, silk
Flannel,
siskin, and
muster-
devilliers

Hose
Points

Piked shoes
Cloaks
Broadcloth
Hoods

Hats *of*
beaver
Feathers
Hair
Colours

39

Edward III (1327-77)

1350

2

1340

3

1360-70

4

lower class

5

1330 -50

1

6

7

8

1340-50

EDWARD III (1327-77)

Women's Fashions

OMEN'S faces were framed in wide, square-shaped headdresses, and the ruffled veil made its appearance. The gown was called the cote-hardie.

A close-fitting under-tunic called the kirtle was always worn. The long **Kirtle** sleeves and tight bodice are seen in Figs. 2 and 3; it was put on over the smock, and unmarried women often wore it without the over-gown.

The gown, like the male supertunic, was called the cote-hardie. The row of buttons **Cote-hardie** down the front (Figs. 1, 4) and the long sleeves and tippets were identical. The dress **Buttons and** was tight down to the hips, hanging in heavy folds to the ground, and the neck was **tippets** cut low, leaving the shoulders bare (Fig. 1). Small vertical slits, called fitchets, were **Fitchets** made in the front of the cote-hardie, so that the purse hanging on the girdle underneath was accessible. Aprons were worn by poor women (Fig. 5 and Plate II). **Aprons**

The sides of the sideless surcoat (p. 37) were so much cut away that only a small **Sideless** panel was left front and back (Figs. 2, 3). These centre panels from the neck to the **surcoat** hip were frequently made of fur with a jewelled band down the front instead of mere buttons (Fig. 2). This gown was worn with little alteration throughout the century, even poor women wearing it in a more simple form (Fig. 5). The new silks and satins **Silk, satin** were used. Taffeta and scarlet cloth for the rich as before; flannel (of fine linen), soft woollen cloths, linens, and russet were also general.

Full cloaks, and sometimes hoods, were used for travelling; the narrower cloak **Cloaks** fastened with rich cords was for State functions (Figs. 2, 4, and Plate I).

The plaits of hair were generally arranged longer, forming a square frame for the **Hair** face (Fig. 1). The wealthy women had these plaits confined in a golden, silver, or embroidered 'tube' on either side of the face, suspended from a narrow band worn round the head (Fig. 6, or, for Court wear, Fig. 2). Veils and wimples were in fashion **Veils** (Figs. 3, 6, 7, 8, and Plate I), and made of a new fine transparent silk for the noblewoman.

The ruffled veil, also seen from c. 1350, consisted of several semicircular pieces of fine *Ruffled veil* linen; the straight edges were pleated or ruffled together, forming either a frame round the face, as in Fig. 4, or a smaller style, only curving over the top of the head; the hanging ends at the back were sometimes ruffled as well.

Buckles, brooches, girdles, etc., were very rich, being made of gold and silver, **Jewellery** set with precious stones. Copper, brass, and wrought iron were also used.

Gold and silver tissue for royalty, new bright tan, and flame colour for nobles **Colours** of high rank, also scarlet, murrey (deep purple-red), greens, blues, red, tawny, red-browns, and greys.

Richard II (1377-99)

1383

1399

merchant

peasant

1   2   3   4   5   6   7

8   9   galoches or pattens   riding-habit

10

RICHARD II (1377–99)

Men's Fashions

THOUGH the fashions of the preceding reign were still worn, great changes took place between 1380 and 1390, when there was a new eccentric cut of men's garments with a definite German influence. There were also Franco-Burgundian novelties of folly-bells and jewelled collars.

In 1380 a very long, full-skirted gown called the houppelande was introduced (Figs. 2, 3, 6), and worn by both sexes. The very high neck reached right up to the ears and had a rich turned-over border. The skirts, slit at the front or sides, were of varying lengths, and fell in carefully arranged folds. The long, trailing skirt was generally kept for more formal occasions (Fig. 3). The waist was higher than before. The sleeves hung very wide and long (Figs. 2, 3, 6). *Houppelande* · Sleeves

Towards the close of the reign the 'bagpipe' sleeve appeared; it hung full like the other sleeve, but it was shaped up to a small cuff at the wrist (Figs. 4, 5). *Bagpipe sleeve*

The skirts, sleeves, and even the neck-borders were dagged (Fig. 6). Dagging

Only the very long, tight sleeves of the gypon were visible (Figs. 1, 2, 6). Gypon

The cote-hardie, buttoned over the padded gypon, was cut very short and tight with the neck and sleeves of the houppelande (Figs. 1, 4). Silk, satin, frieze (thick woollen cloth), fustian (p. 31), fine woollen cloths, taffeta for linings, and russet for the poorer men were used. Cote-hardie · *Frieze*

The hose now reached from toe to hip, and were attached to the gypon by means of the eyelet holes and 'points' (laces with 'tag' ends). Red hose were fashionable. Hose

The front fork of the hose was covered by a triangular piece, called the cod-piece (Figs. 1, 4). This was worn till about 1570; it was also fastened up with points. *Cod-piece*

The long, pointed toes of the shoes became very exaggerated, and by the end of the reign were sometimes curled back and fastened to the leg below the knee (Figs. 4, 8). Soled hose were still worn (Figs. 1, 4). Piked shoes

By 1390 galoches, or pattens, were strapped to the feet in bad weather (Fig. 9). *Galoches*

The lower classes still wore the hood in the usual way (Fig. 7). The new fashion of wearing it as a hat (p. 35), with the lirapipe sometimes twisted round the head, was popular. It was called the chaperon (Figs. 2, 6), and could be worn over the hood. Hoods · Chaperon

The latter half of this period saw different-shaped tall-crowned hats with rolled brims (Figs. 1, 3), or beaver hats with turned-up brims (Fig. 5). Hats

The hair was 'bobbed' until 1395, when it was curled outward in a thick roll covering the tips of the ears, and falling lower round the nape of the neck (Figs. 1, 4). Pointed beards were sometimes seen (Figs. 3, 4). Hair

Jewelled collars and folly-bells were worn (Fig. 3). These bells were also hung on little chains from the girdle; the purse and dagger were carried (Fig. 6). *Novelties* · Purse and dagger

Colours are on women's page, p. 45. Particoloured clothes remained in fashion. Colours

43

Richard II (1377-99)

1

2 middle-class

peasant 3

4

13

nobility

RICHARD II (1377–99)

Women's Fashions

THE sideless surcoat, kirtle, and cote-hardie, all with low necks, continued to be worn until the end of the century. The houppelande came into fashion in the 1390's.

The kirtle, or under-tunic, with long, tight sleeves, remained unaltered (Figs. 1, 2, 5). The smock, or chemise, was of linen, or silk for the wealthy (Fig. 1). | **Kirtle** **Smock**

The graceful cote-hardie (Fig. 2), sometimes buttoned down the front as in the previous reign, was still quite fashionable. The upper classes had the sleeves closely buttoned from elbow to wrist as before (Plate I). | **Cote-hardie**

The low side-openings of the sideless surcoat were cut the same, but the skirt was often made of different material and gathered on to the front and back panels and side-pieces (Figs. 1, 5). | **Sideless surcoat**

At the close of the reign women adopted the houppelande worn by the men, and wore it with very little alteration, the high neck and long sleeves being identical. The belt was high at the waist (Fig. 4 and Plate III), or it could be worn unbelted. | *Houppelande*

Silks, satin, taffeta, fustian, embroidered materials, fine woollen cloths, thick cloth (frieze), serge, and russet were used. | **Frieze**

The hair at first was still parted in the centre with the two plaited coils, forming a square-shaped frame for the face. A narrow band was worn round the head, or the coronet for Court wear, with the embroidered or jewelled caul (Fig. 5). | **Hair**

The long-shaped form of headdress, fashionable in the reign before, was now replaced by a round variety set higher on the head over the ears; note the slightly rounded shape worn with the straight side-plaits (Fig. 5), and the more rounded form made of coarser wire, with a jewelled band (Fig. 1). A wide, ornamented, padded roll, made of silk or satin, called the chaplet, was fashionable with the houppelande (Fig. 4). | **Headdress** *Chaplet*

A short veil was worn with most headdresses (Fig. 4); it usually hung at the back only; often more than one veil was used (Plate I). | **Veils**

The wimple still covered the throat of the middle-class and poorer woman (Figs. 2, 3), but it was no longer fashionable among the upper classes. | **Wimple**

The pointed shoes were similar to those worn by the men, though, of course, not so extreme. | **Shoes**

Scarlet, greens, and blue, also red and white (the King's colours), and blue and white (Lancastrian), red hose were fashionable for men; purple, black, russets, and greys were also worn. | **Colours**

45

Henry IV (1399-1413)

1

2

3

4

5

6

7

11

HENRY IV (1399–1413)

Men's Fashions

EXCEPT for a few small alterations, men's fashions remained very much the same as before. Velvet was worn by the nobility, and new silks from abroad.

The folds of the houppelande were arranged carefully under the girdle, and the long skirts were closed all the way round or open only at the sides (Figs. 4, 5). The shorter houppelande hung to the calf (Fig. 2). A loose-hanging gown was sometimes worn by elderly men (Fig. 1). The neck was high during the first few years (Figs. 3, 6, 7), but by 1410 it was noticeably lower and slit down the front (Figs. 2, 4, 5, and Plate II).

The long hanging sleeves, fur-lined or dagged, were still seen (Figs. 2, 5), but the bagpipe sleeve was more popular (Figs. 3, 4).

Extra shoulder-pieces with dagged edges made their appearance (Figs. 4, 6, 7), and sometimes the sleeves were pleated into the armhole (Fig. 7).

The padded gypon, to which the hose were fastened, was rarely seen.

In 1405 the pleats of the short cote-hardie were padded and stitched into place, front and back (Fig. 3); it had the neck and sleeves of the houppelande. The fastening was side or front lacing (Figs. 3, 6), buttons appearing less often. Velvet was now used by the nobility, also silks, satin, and fine woollen cloths. The thicker cloths, serge, frieze, and broadcloth were for the outer garments; woollen cloths and russet were for the poor. The wealthy used fur for lining or trimming (Plate II).

The hose were still fastened on the hips to the gypon. Long soled-hose were quite general, and the toes were less pointed (Fig. 3).

The exaggerated pointed toes went out of fashion. Long boots that fitted the leg to well above the knee were worn for travelling. In 1410 short boots to the calf were laced or buckled on the outer side to fit the leg (Fig. 2).

Cloaks were no longer used by the upper classes.

The fashionable way of dressing the hair in 1410 is best described as the 'bowl' crop. The head was shaved up at the back and sides (sometimes to above the ears), and the hair, with the ends curled slightly under, looked like a cap on the head (Fig. 3). Beards went out of fashion by the end of the reign.

The converted hood, now the chaperon, continued in favour (Figs. 1, 2, 5).

From 1394 to 1415 soft high-crowned hats with a rolled or turned-up brim were fashionable (Fig. 6), also another variety with the crown flopping over the brim (Fig. 4). A form of head-covering worn by men and women was the round chaplet, usually made up of dark material cut up or dagged into small leaf-shapes (Fig. 7).

Personal adornments were very elaborate, and the purses hung at the waist were bigger and more richly decorated (Fig. 5).

Colours on p. 49.

Marginal notes: Houppelande · Sleeves · *Shoulder-pieces* · Gypon · Cote-hardie · Velvet · Hose · Shoes · Cloaks · Hair · *'Bowl' crop* · Chaperon · Hats · Chaplet · Jewellery, etc. · Colours

Henry IV (1399–1413)

1

2

3

4

1410

1405

5

6

7

HENRY IV (1399-1413)

Women's Fashions

THE outstanding changes in the women's fashions were the increasing width of all forms of headdresses, the lower neck of the houppelande, and the higher waistline. Velvet was worn by noblewomen, and new richly patterned silks.

The houppelande was now more generally used, and the folds of the long, trailing skirt were carefully arranged under the high-waisted belt (Figs. 2, 3). The high neck hitherto worn (Fig. 7) was frequently slit down the front (Plate III), and then made much lower (Figs. 2, 3). By the end of the reign the throat was bared, and the neck was V-shaped in the front, with a wide linen collar set flat across the shoulders (Fig. 6). The sleeves of the houppelande became so wide that they sometimes touched the ground (Fig. 3). The gown was frequently fur-lined or trimmed (Plate II). **Houppelande**

Sleeves

The long fitting cote-hardie was seen for a few years (Figs. 1, 4), and the sleeves remained as before, covering the hand to the knuckles; sometimes long, graceful streamers hung to the ground from small, padded shoulder-pieces (Fig. 4). **Cote-hardie**

Velvet was used by noblewomen, also fine, elaborately brocaded silks and velvets from the Continent (Plate II); and silks, satin, and fine cloths of wool, also thick woollen cloths (frieze), and russets were used. **Velvet** *Brocades*

Cloaks for State wear were often circular in shape and fastened across the front with cords or jewelled clasps (Fig. 1 and Plate III). These, and sometimes the dresses, were often decorated with the wearer's coat-of-arms. Velvet for the nobles, serge, and broadcloth were used. **Cloaks**

The hair was dressed wide up on either side of the head (Fig. 6), and from 1400 to 1410 it was arranged above the ears (seen under the caul, Plate III and Figs. 1, 3, 4, 5). Small veils that were draped over the head of the more elderly women (Fig. 7, or, for informal wear, Fig. 6) followed the current fashions. Light veils were also worn with many of the fashionable headdresses (Figs. 1, 2, 3). **Hair**

Veils

The decorated roll (Fig. 2) was still seen for a year or two; after then it became much smaller and was set flat on the head (Fig. 5). By the end of the reign there was a marked dip in the centre of all forms of headwear (Figs. 3, 4, 7), and we have the first signs of the horned (Figs. 1, 7) and heart-shaped headdresses (Fig. 4 and Plate II). **Headdress** *Horned and heart-shaped*

Metal (gold, silver, etc.) collars made up of the letter 'S' were worn by the nobility of both sexes (Fig. 5). The exact meaning of the 'S' is not known, but it has been suggested that it may stand for the initial letter of Henry IV's motto 'Souveraine', which he had borne while Earl of Derby. **Jewellery** *'S' collars*

Scarlet, crimson, greens, and watchet (light greenish blue) remained in favour. **Colours**

Henry v (1413 - 22)

1

2

3

12

HENRY V (1413–22)

Men's Fashions

THERE were no new outstanding features for men, and the exaggerated fashions of Henry IV's time died out.

The houppelande was worn a great deal, and the folds were often sewn into place both front and back, under the low-waisted girdle. The neck, slightly lower, was occasionally open a little way down the front (Fig. 1). The skirts were not open at the sides so much as before, and were sometimes closed all the way round (Figs. 2, 3). *Houppelande*

The wide type of sleeve (Fig. 2) was retained for State functions until nearly 1450; the bagpipe sleeve (Fig. 3) was more common for general wear, but it was gradually replaced by a smaller, though by no means fitting, sleeve (Fig. 1). Fur linings and trimmings were very fashionable. Velvet, silks, satins, and the fine scarlet cloth were used by the nobility, also fine woollen cloths, fustian (silky like velvet), coarser cloths, and russets were worn. Serge, broadcloth, and frieze were for outer garments and winter wear. *Sleeve*

The gypon was still worn under the cote-hardie or houppelande, though it was seldom seen. *Gypon*

The short fitting cote-hardie was the same as in the previous reign, with the sleeve and neck fashions borrowed from the houppelande. The skirt was a little longer. It did not, however, seem to be so popular as the long, stately garment. *Cote-hardie*

The hose were still attached to the gypon with points (see p. 43). From 1420 particoloured hose (legs of different colours) were no longer fashionable. *Hose*

Shoes, soled hose, and the long fitting travelling-boots were unaltered. *Shoes*

The long cloak was seldom used except for travelling. *Cloaks*

The 'bowl-crop' fashion of cutting the hair was still very popular. Beards were out of fashion and were rarely seen until 1535. *Hair*

The chaperon and the various soft-crowned hats of the previous reign continued (Figs. 1, 2). The purse and dagger were worn on the belt (Figs. 1, 3). *Hats, purse, and dagger*

Colours are given on the women's page of this reign, p. 53. *Colours*

Henry V (1413-22)

1

3

4 nobility

6

1415

2

5

middle class

HENRY V (1413–22)

Women's Fashions

EXCEPT for even wider headdresses women's fashions were almost unchanged. The houppelande still had the very high waistline, but the high neck was not seen any more after 1415. It was replaced by the lower V-shaped neck with the flat linen collar that was introduced at the end of Henry IV's reign (Figs. 2, 3, 5); this linen collar was frequently worn double. The wide sleeves were inclined to be even longer than before; they were often fur-lined.

The sleeves of the undergown, or kirtle, were laced up from the wrist (Plate III).

The gown, or one-time cote-hardie, was still worn by some of the elderly middle-class women (Fig. 6); being fitting down to the hips as before, very unlike the full, high-belted houppelande. Noblewomen used the silks, satin, velvet, and the fine cloth of scarlet wool. Fustian (similar to velvet, only slightly cheaper), fine woollen cloths, coarser cloths, russet, and linens were used. Neck openings were laced across.

Narrow cloaks were worn with full Court dress (Fig. 4). For travelling, women wore full cloaks with shoulder-capes, sometimes having hoods attached.

The hair was generally hidden under the various net-coverings throughout this period. Until 1420 young girls still occasionally wore their hair loose.

Though width was the dominant feature, some headdresses had quite a strong upward movement. This was very noticeable in the roll-shaped headdress of Fig. 3 (see also Fig. 4, p. 48); also a slight tendency was seen in the very wide fashion of Fig. 4. The head-covering of Fig. 5, with the shaped, decorated roll crowning the head, was quite general, and it was sometimes even wider; the more pointed shape with the short veil (Figs. 1, 2) was also popular among the upper classes. Elderly middle-class women wore quite fashionably arranged linen head-coverings, and if widows they often wore the wimple as well (Fig. 6).

In 1415 lawn (fine, almost transparent linen) was mentioned.

Scarlet and bright tan were still worn by the nobility; greens, blues, red, deep purple-red, black, tawny, russets, and grey continued as before.

Houppelande

Sleeves

Kirtle
Gown

Cloaks

Hair

Headdress
Heart-shaped
    and horned

Lawn
Colours

Henry VI (1422-61)

1

1455
-60

2

1440
-45

3

1437

4

1455

5

6

7

c

b

a

13

HENRY VI (1422–61)

Men's Fashions

DURING this reign the houppelande lost two of its most outstanding features: the high neck and wide sleeves. Chaperons were now made differently. Damask was first mentioned in 1430.

The extreme high collar of the houppelande disappeared; it was now cut much lower with a small V-shaped opening in the front (Fig. 3). By 1440 it was distinctly low-necked, and generally trimmed with fur (Fig. 5, and p. 58, Fig. 3). The gown with the open front (Fig. 3) was not so fashionable after 1440, when the skirts were shorter and of varying lengths (Figs. 4, 5 and Plate II). The houppelande was girdled even lower on the hips, especially during the last ten years of this reign (Figs. 1, 4). The bagpipe sleeve, fast becoming old-fashioned, was much smaller (Fig. 3). The general sleeve of the period was fairly loose, being full and gathered at the shoulder, with fitting fur-trimmed cuffs (Figs. 4, 5 and Plate II); towards the end of the reign plain wide cuffs were fairly popular (Fig. 1).

Houppelande

Sleeves

The collar of the gypon was made higher, and showed above the neck of the upper garment (Figs. 1, 2, 4, 5). Fustian (like velvet) was used a great deal.

Gypon

The cote-hardie was worn longer, and it still had the neck and sleeves of the houppelande (Fig. 2).

Cote-hardie

Damask (a richly patterned silk, originally made in Damascus) and a soft silky cloth (mixture of silk and fine hair) were new materials for royalty and noblemen; velvet, silk, satin, and various woollen cloths were in use as before; in 1423 Holland (fine quality linen for shirts, etc.) was used.

Damask

Holland

The hose still reached to the hip, where they were fastened to the gypon.

Hose

In 1440 the toes of the shoes, boots, and soled hose were made pointed again; and in 1450 the long travelling-boots reaching up to the thigh were adopted by the upper classes for general wear; they were buckled to fit the leg and had coloured turned-over tops (Figs. 4, 5).

Shoes

The short 'bowl crop' was still in vogue, but between 1450 and 1460 the hair was allowed to grow longer (Fig. 4); after 1460 the long 'bob' returned to favour.

Hair

The fashion of wearing the hood as a hat and calling it the 'chaperon' now developed still farther. It was made in three separate parts and sewn together (Fig. 7): (a) the lirapipe, (b) the padded roundlet, and (c) the cape part, or gorget (Plate II).

Chaperon

Tall-crowned hats began to appear during the last few years of the reign (Fig. 4). Countrymen still retained the old-fashioned hat and the hood (Fig. 6).

Hats

Colours are given on p. 57.

Colours

Henry VI (1422-61)

1445
1

1440-45
3

2

1423
4

1433
5

1450-60
6

cour-
dre

7

1431

1451
8

middle-
class

140
9

HENRY VI (1422–61)

Women's Fashions

HIGHER headdresses and even lower necks were affected by the wealthy lady of fashion. Long, trailing sleeves disappeared. Damask was worn (Plate II).

The high neck and long, wide sleeves which once characterized the houppelande vanished during this reign. The bodice was tiny and fitting, with a very high waist, the skirt was long and full, and trailed on the ground for Court wear (Figs. 3, 6). The neck at first was rounded or V-shaped with a linen or fur collar (Figs. 4, 5); by 1440 it was deepened back and front down to the high-waisted belt, baring the shoulders (Figs. 1, 3, 6). For more general wear the neck of the gown was made in a deep 'V' at the front, sometimes to below the girdle, showing the undergarments, which were cut in a more moderate fashion (Figs. 8, 9). The long, hanging sleeve was worn for a year or two (Fig. 4), and the bagpipe sleeve continued (Fig. 5); then a smaller sleeve, quite loose-fitting, with either a small or a wide cuff, replaced it (Figs. 1, 3, 9); later the sleeves were made tight down to the wrist (Fig. 6). Fur trimmings and linings were popular. Damask, velvet, silken cloths, and satins were worn by the rich; woollen cloths, flannel (made of wool), and russets were used by the poorer people.

Eyebrows were plucked, also the hair, so that it was almost entirely concealed beneath the headdress (Plates II, III).

The roll-shaped headdress was now developed to the fullest extent, and it was generally known as the heart-shaped headdress. The decorative roll, low over the forehead, curled up on either side of the head in quite a variety of ways, being at first more rounded (Figs. 4, 5), then pointed in the front (Fig. 1), and finally curved steeply up in a sharp U-shape (Figs. 3, 9). The side-pieces over the ears were generally made of richly decorated wire or net-like coverings; sometimes they were of the same embroidered materials as the roll (Fig. 3). The long streamer, or lirapipe, was often adapted from the male chaperon (Fig. 1). The high, pointed headdress with the fine gauze veil supported on a wire frame was quite general on the Continent, but in England was worn only by the extremely fashionable noblewomen (Fig. 6).

A veil with the edge softly frilled was often worn over the heart-shaped headdress instead of the roll (Fig. 2). Middle-class and elderly women or widows usually had shaped headdresses of linen with a short veil at the back (Figs. 7, 8). The pleated barbe, not unlike a form of wimple, continued to be worn by widows throughout this century. A lady of rank, such as a baroness, wore it above the chin (Fig. 7), otherwise it reached to below the chin.

Richly patterned materials were often worn by men and women of rank. No new colours are mentioned. See p. 53.

Gown

Sleeve

Damask
Flannel
Hair

Heart-shaped
  Headdress

Hennin

Veils

Colours, etc.

See p. 53.

Edward IV (1461-83)

1   2   3   4   5   6   7 1475

8

14

EDWARD IV (1461–83)

Men's Fashions

THE influence of Burgundy on English fashions became even more noticeable. Hats replaced the chaperon; the gypon was renamed the 'doublet', and the cote-hardie the 'jerkin'. Hose now reached to the waist.

No longer called the gypon, the doublet was little changed. The front was still *Doublet* well padded, and only long, tight sleeves and high neck were visible, as it was hidden under the over-garment. Made of silks, satin, and velvets for the wealthy.

The jerkin retained the main features of the cote-hardie, being well fitting, with *Jerkin* the folds carefully padded and stitched front and back (Fig. 4). The neck was low, and the shirt was sometimes seen, as in Fig. 2. The length of the jerkin varied, being sometimes short to the hips (Fig. 4), or longer, half-way between hip and knee. It was girdled round the hips.

At first the sleeves remained as before (p. 54, Fig. 2), but later they increased in *Sleeves* length and width, often having a slit in the front, so that they could hang free from shoulder to knee (Fig. 4), or be loosely tied together at the back, as in Fig. 6.

Both long and short gowns were worn. The long type retained the full-skirted effect *Gown* of the houppelande, with the folds carefully padded and sewn into position (Figs. 1, 3, 6). The low neck was often V-shaped in the front (Fig. 3). The short gown, like the long one, was closed all the way round, but it was not girdled, so that it hung free from shoulder to mid-thigh or hip (Fig. 2).

The sleeves of both gowns were full, especially at the shoulder, where they were *Sleeves* gathered and often padded, giving a very broad-shouldered appearance (Figs. 1, 4, 6). The separate hanging sleeves were very fashionable (Fig. 6). Nobles wore velvets, figured satins, and damask. Woollen cloths, serge, frieze, and broadcloth were used.

From 1475 the hose covered the legs from toe to waist, where they were attached *Hose* to the doublet with points (see p. 39); cod-pieces were worn as before (see p. 43).

During the first twenty years the toes of all footwear were very pointed. Tall boots *Piked shoes* with turned-over tops remained in fashion. Coloured leathers were used. In bad weather thick wooden soles called pattens were strapped to the feet (Fig. 8). *Pattens*

In 1465 quite long hair was fashionable for the dandy (Fig. 2), but a medium 'bob' *Hair* was usual.

The chaperon was now worn only by elderly or professional men. Hats of beaver *Hats* and felt were of many different shapes; high or low crowned with wide or rolled *Felt hats* brims. A low-crowned hat was worn with a wide, turned-up brim, which was fastened with a jewelled brooch (Fig. 7). Metal bands, sometimes jewelled, were worn round hats, and ostrich plumes came into fashion (Fig. 4). The lirapipe of the chaperon remained for a few years, being sometimes attached to the brim of the beaver hat (Figs. 1, 3). Colours are shown on the women's page of this reign, p. 61. *Colours*

Edward IV (1461-83)

1
1470

2

3

4

5
1479

6
1480

7

8

EDWARD IV (1461–83)

Women's Fashions

THE new 'butterfly' headdress was the latest fashion for women (Plate III).
The gown with the tiny bodice, high waist, and full skirt was hardly altered;   **Gowns**
but the tight sleeves were now so long that they almost covered the hand.
Though the high waist was more general, gowns with a low waist were sometimes
seen (Fig. 5); also for Court wear a low-waisted dress was worn (Fig. 3), with a faint
suggestion of the sideless surcoat—an echo of the fashion of 1350. A low, rounded neck
(Fig. 5) sometimes replaced the deep V-shape of Figs. 2, 4, and on more simple dresses
the round opening was sometimes filled in with a plain, dark material (Fig. 8); square
necks showing the top of the under-dress were quite common (Fig. 7). Noblewomen
wore damasks, many rich varieties of velvet, silks, and satin, also taffeta and soft woollen
cloths. Coarser woollen cloths, frieze, flannel (of wool), russet, and linens were used by
the poorer people.

Long, narrow, richly lined cloaks were worn with Court dress (Fig. 3), and large   **Cloaks**
circular cloaks were for general use, of velvet, broadcloth, frieze, and woollen cloths.

The hair, plucked back from the forehead, was coiled up on the back of the head   **Hair**
and bound with black ribbon or velvet (see the painting, Plate III); the cap-shape was
then pinned to this and held securely in position.

The heart-shaped headdress was seen during the first fifteen to twenty years (Figs. 2,   **Headdress**
3); also the horned (Fig. 1) was worn tilted well back on the head; this backward
movement became very characteristic of the head fashions during the next few years.
The very tall Continental hennin (Fig. 4), which was only worn in England by the
extremist copying Burgundian fashions, formed the foundation for a short variety that
became quite common (Fig. 7). It was usually made of dark material. Note also the
turned-back front- and side-pieces of Figs. 7, 8.

From this shorter variety another and more decorative style appeared (Figs. 5, 6).
It was worn right at the back of the head and was covered with a fine gauze veil held
out on wires, and was called the 'butterfly' headdress. During the following reign it   *Butterfly*
was the most fashionable form of headwear. The small loop occasionally seen on the   *headdress*
forehead in the front of these sloped-back fashions (Figs. 7, 8) was probably used for
arranging the angle of the erection.

Wealthy women wore wide jewelled collars round the throat (Plate III).   **Jewellery**

Gold and silver tissue continued in favour for royalty; scarlet, crimson, black,   **Colours**
greens, blue, tawny, and russet were popular. There is no record of any new colours.

Edward v – Richard iii (1483–85)

1

2

3

15

EDWARD V—RICHARD III (1483–85)

Men's Fashions

THE latest fashion was to slash the sleeve of the doublet, showing the fine linen shirt underneath. This was the first appearance of 'slashing'. High-crowned hats were no longer worn.

When the doublet was worn without the jerkin (Fig. 3) the front was left open almost to the waist, displaying the shirt; the lower part was generally laced loosely together; also crochets and loops (hooks and eyes) may have been used.

A stomacher, or plackard (Fig. 3), was often worn between the shirt and the doublet so that it showed at the laced opening. Women retained a form of this front-piece into the eighteenth century. The girdle was set fairly low on the hips with the doublet finishing just below (Fig. 3).

The sleeves of the doublet were still fairly full, with a fitting cuff.

There were sometimes one or more 'slashes' in the sleeve at the elbow, or between the elbow and wrist, and the fine shirt-sleeve was puffed out through these slits (Fig. 3). Rich materials were used for the doublet: satin, damask, etc.

Now that the shirt was so often displayed, it became much finer in quality and was beautifully embroidered at the neckband, black and red silk with gold thread being very fashionable colours for the noblemen.

The jerkin was longer than the doublet, generally reaching to mid-thigh (Fig. 1), and its sleeves could also be slashed. The neck was cut fairly low and square at first, showing the shirt (the neck and sleeves of the jerkin can be seen under the gown of Fig. 2). The materials were velvet, damask, etc.

Long or short gowns were fashionable; both types hung in heavy folds, and opened down the front with facings or broad collars of fur or a contrasting material.

The sleeves were long and wide, and were slashed in the front so that they could hang free from the shoulder (Figs. 1, 2, 3). They were made of satin, velvet, damask, or cloth of gold lined with velvet for royalty. Frieze, serge, and broadcloth were used by middle and lower classes.

The hose were fastened to the doublet as before, at the waist. The cod-piece continued.

By the end of the reign the shoe with the pointed toe (Fig. 3) was replaced by a more moderately shaped style.

Long 'bobbed' hair remained in fashion.

A low-crowned hat with a turned-up brim that had been worn in the preceding reign was now the fashionable headwear; a small part of the brim was generally cut away in the front and laced across with gold or silken cords.

Colours are shown on p. 65.

Doublet
Crochets and loops
Stomacher, or plackard

Sleeves
Slashing

Shirt and *embroidered neckband*
Jerkin

Gown

Sleeves

Hose

Shoes

Hair
Hats

Colours

Edward v – Richard III (1483-85)

1
1484

2

3

4

EDWARD V—RICHARD III (1483–85)

Women's Fashions

THE 'butterfly' headdress was very popular during these few years.

The graceful gown, usually high-waisted, remained unaltered, the bodice being small and fitting, with the skirt hanging in heavy folds to the ground. Sometimes the pleated skirt was sewn separately to the tiny bodice (Fig. 4). The neck was rounded and fairly low, with either wide or narrow collars of rich fabric or embroidery (Figs. 2, 4). Velvet or fur trimmings were popular, and often a deep band of fur was worn at the hem (Plate III). Velvets, silks, satins, damask, and fine, soft woollen cloths were used by the upper classes; frieze, coarser cloths, and russet were general for the lower classes. *Gown*

Sleeves were very fitting, usually with cuffs matching the trimming or collar, at the neck; at times these cuffs extended over the hand to the knuckles (Plate III). *Sleeves*

The petticoat, or under-dress, was seen only at the front of some of the low-necked dresses (Figs. 1, 3, 4), and the fine linen or silken smock was occasionally visible. *Under-dress and smock*

The hair was taken straight back from the face into the round-shaped headdress. The forehead was still plucked, also the eyebrows. *Hair*

Though the round shape of the butterfly headdress was decorated in a variety of ways, it will be noticed they were all of a very similar length, and were tilted right back off the head at about the same angle. The fine linen or gauze veils that were draped from the centre of the forehead were held out on wires or canes, and they gave the individual touch to these headdresses. One can still see today, on some of the monumental brasses, many fine examples of this fashion (Plate III). *Butterfly headdress*

The extra strip of gauze veiling the forehead in Fig. 4 was retained in the smaller and heavier 'hood' shape of the following reign, and formed the basis of the front-piece on the 'gable' hood (p. 68). Fine jewelled collars were worn (Figs. 1, 4). *Jewellery*

The shoes were very similar to those worn by the men. *Shoes*

Purple, green, crimson, and black were worn, also deep blue, tawny, and russet. The darker colours were used more by the men. *Colours*

1 2 **1495** 3 4 **Henry VII (1485~1509)** 5

16

HENRY VII (1485–1509)

Men's Fashions

ENGLISH fashions were influenced by France and Italy.
Wide round-toed shoes made their appearance.
The doublet, still with the low neck, was sometimes very short, reaching **Doublet**
only to the waist (Fig. 2). The front was often slashed, with the shirt puffed out between;
the plackard covered the front opening (Figs. 4, 5). **Plackard**

The sleeves were full and slashed as before. One long slash, revealing the shirt **Sleeves**
from elbow to wrist, was sometimes affected (Fig. 2), and a number of small slashes
down the length of the arm were not uncommon (Fig. 5). The materials were silks,
satin, damask, and velvet, while woollen cloths were used by the poorer people.

The neck of the shirt was often made quite low; it was still richly embroidered. **Shirt**

The jerkin, worn over the doublet, was made either with or without sleeves. If **Jerkin**
it had sleeves they were long, and wide, and slashed in the front, so that they could
hang loosely from the shoulder, as in Fig. 4, p. 58. The neck was cut the same as the
doublet. The jerkin was longer, with a full skirt reaching to just above the knee, and
it was girdled round the waist.

The gown was of varying lengths as before, though the short type was favoured **Gown**
by the dandy (Figs. 2, 3). They could hang loose or were belted at the waist. Wide
fur facings were fashionable; these broadened out at the shoulder (Figs. 2, 3, 5), with a
deep square-shaped collar at the back (Fig. 1). The sleeves, slashed from shoulder to
wrist, often hung very long. The same materials were used as before.

The hose still reached to the waist, where they were fastened to the doublet (Fig. 2). **Hose**
The dandy sometimes had them striped or particoloured, or the top part covering
the hips was made of a different material or colour and occasionally slashed. This was
the first sign of the 'trunk' hose. From 1495 to 1505 short, loose stockings were some- *Short*
times worn over the hose (Fig. 2). Hose were made of fine cloth or silk, or even velvet *stockings*
cut on the cross.

The pointed shoe was replaced by a wide, flat, round-toed shoe (Figs. 2, 3, 5), **Shoes**
and made of leather, silk, cloth, or velvet. Tasselled purses hung from the belt (Fig. 3). **Purses**

The hair was worn longer down to the shoulders. **Hair**

Small, soft-crowned hats became very common, and the turned-up brim was **Hats**
fastened with a brooch (Fig. 2). By 1505 the brim was sloped outward, as in Fig. 4.
Fur, velvet, leather (Fig. 1), or woollen hats were seen. A very wide-brimmed hat,
decorated with coloured plumes, was occasionally worn. It was fastened under the
chin (Fig. 3), or slung over the shoulder with a wide ribbon. Small caps of silk, velvet,
or cloth, and also embroidered materials, were worn under the large hat.

Colours are given on p. 69. **Colours**

1

1495

2

3

4

HENRY VII (1485–1509)

Women's Fashions

DARK hoods became the usual headwear, and the 'butterfly' headdresses were seen no more. The high-waisted gown with the rounded neckline went out of fashion.

Though the low-necked gown with the high waist was worn until 1490, the gown with the square-shaped neck and more normal waistline eventually replaced it (Figs. 1, 3). The bodice was fitting, and generally had a fairly high neck; the opening was sometimes filled in with a dark material (Fig. 1) or fine linen (Figs. 2, 3), or both (Fig. 4); when the neck of the gown was cut square and low, as in Fig. 1, or up in the centre, as in Fig. 4, the other material was usually sewn to the gown itself (see also p. 72, Fig. 2, and p. 76, Fig. 2). A narrow sash, knotted at the front, was frequently used instead of a belt (Fig. 4). Skirts were full, sometimes having a long train at the back that was fastened up to the waist, showing the rich lining of fur, silk, or velvet (Fig. 1). *Gown*

Sash

The sleeves were small and tight at first (Fig. 3), sometimes with pointed cuffs and the sleeve slashed up to the elbow (Fig. 4); later, very wide, richly lined sleeves were worn with the long, trailing dress (Fig. 1). Velvet and fine woollen cloths were used a great deal, also silks, satin, and coarser cloths, and russet as before. Sleeves

A simple, sideless gown was still used for State functions (Fig. 2, see also p. 40).

The skirt of the under-dress was occasionally displayed when the gown was caught up at the back, as in Fig. 1. Aprons were worn by the middle and lower classes. Under-dress / Aprons

The hair was seen again in the front of the hood, and it was parted in the centre (Fig. 1). Hair

Plain rounded hoods (as women's headdresses were now called) had a full hanging piece at the back and a coloured lining turned back from the face (Fig. 1). The sides were often slit part way up with the front-pieces brought forward over the shoulder; this became general after 1490. A simple round hood with pointed side-pieces was also worn (Fig. 4, note similarity of Fig. 7, p. 60, and Fig. 4, p. 64). The English 'gable' hood with the stiffened, shaped front and dark drapery hanging at the back (Figs. 2, 3) became very popular, and was worn by all classes until about 1550; both upper and lower classes frequently had the drapery hanging from a pointed style (Fig. 2, p. 72, also Fig. 2, p. 76). The hood was usually made of black material with a small cap of linen, velvet, or gold tissue underneath, the undercap having a very decorative border. *Hoods* / *Gable hood* / Undercap

The tailored stockings were gartered above the knee with a tied or buckled band of material. Stockings

Greens, reds, tawny, russets, blue-green, and grey were worn, no fresh colours being introduced during this reign. Colours

Henry VIII (1509-47)

merchant 1
1525

2   1528   1519   3   4   5

merchants
son
6
1525

17

HENRY VIII (1509–47)

Men's Fashions

BROAD shoulders, flat hats, and square-toed shoes were outstanding features. The doublet, worn over the shirt and under the jerkin, generally had a low, square neck until 1530 (Fig. 1); it was then gradually made higher, until by 1540 it formed a narrow collar or band round the throat. The skirt of the doublet was very short at first, but was lengthened later. | Doublet

At times separate carefully pleated skirts called 'bases' (similar to Fig. 6) were made, worn with the doublet. Sleeves were still slashed and fairly full to the wrist. | *Bases* / Sleeves

The materials were velvets, satin, fustian, damask, etc., as before, also calico for the rich. Canvas trimmed with lace was quite usual. | *Calico*

By 1525 the shirt was high round the neck (Fig. 1), gathered into quite a deep band that was tied at the front. Red, black, and gold embroidery was still popular. In 1540 the top of the band was frilled or turned down in a small collar (Figs. 4, 5). | Shirt

The jerkin was made similar to the doublet, sometimes without sleeves, or with the sleeves puffed to the elbow, then fitting down to the wrist (Figs. 1, 6). | Jerkin and sleeves

They were made of velvet, satins, damask, and a 'mock' velvet (of silk and wool, or silk and linen), also woollen cloths. | 'Mock' velvet

Although the hose were made in one garment as before, covering the leg up to the waist, the top part was of different material or colour, and made very full and 'pouched' (Figs. 5, 6) and was often slashed. They were still attached to the doublet at the waist with points. Cod-pieces were much exaggerated. | Hose

The wide, rounded toes gave place to wide, square-toed shoes (Figs. 1, 2, 6), but more rounded and pointed shoes reappeared at the end of the reign (Fig. 5). Slashed toes were quite common (Figs. 1, 4). Boots were worn on horseback. | Shoes / Boots

Long gowns of thick cloth, often faced or lined throughout with fur, were worn by older men (Figs. 1, 2, 3); they frequently had long, full sleeves, slashed in front so that they hung free to below the hem of the gown. Short gowns with sleeves very puffed and full from elbow to shoulder were very fashionable (Figs. 4, 5). | Gowns

The long hair remained until 1530, but from 1525 it was worn much shorter (Fig. 5). | Hair

Faces were clean-shaven until about 1535, when short beards and moustaches returned to favour (Fig. 4). | Beards

By the second half of the reign the soft cap-shape with the turned-up brim (Fig. 2) was worn only by elderly or professional men. Hats with a soft crown and almost flat brim (sometimes called a bonnet), often decorated with an ostrich plume, came into fashion from 1520 (Figs. 4, 5). They were made of fine cloth or velvet, or taffeta from 1530, and black woollen knitted flat hats became general for younger men. | Hats / *Bonnets* / *Knitted flat hats*

Gloves were carried, also fairly tall walking-sticks. Daggers and short swords were worn. Colours are shown on p. 73. | Gloves, etc. / Colours

71

Henry VIII (1509-47)

1530
1

1519
2

3

4

5

1540

6   1530

1520
-43
7

8

9 1541

10

HENRY VIII (1509–47)

Women's Fashions

THE English gable hood, the tight bodice with low, square neckline, long, trailing skirts, and sleeves with huge cuffs were typical of the period.

The bodice was beautifully fitted, being laced, hooked, or pinned at back or front; it had a wide, low, square neckline edged with narrow frilling and sometimes trimmed with pearls (Fig. 1), or embroidered in black silk from *c.* 1530, or later in white cut-work. Smaller neck openings were also seen (Figs. 2, 5). At times the opening was covered as in Figs. 4, 10, and from *c.* 1530 it was often filled in with a dark material, this 'partlet' having a semicircular collar of lace (from 1545) or linen standing up round the throat (Fig. 9). The skirt was long and full, trailing on the ground at first; from *c.* 1530 it was often open in front, displaying the decorative petticoat, was shorter to ground-level all round and smoothly gored from the waist (Fig. 1) instead of gathered. The wide cuffs on the short fitting sleeves were of fur or richly patterned silk, with the separate decorative under-sleeves buttoned or tied with laces to the upper sleeve. The smock sleeves were visible at the wrist, or if the sleeves were slashed (Fig. 1).

Long, hanging girdles were worn (Figs. 2, 5), also the popular knotted sash (Figs. 1, 7).

Gowns were of taffeta, velvet, silk, satin, damask, soft silken cloths, 'mock' velvet, and fine woollen cloths; rich linings were used; the poor wore coarser cloths and russets.

The hair was bound with silks or ribbons into two long tails and wound round the head, crossing in front (Figs. 1, 3, 7). From *c.* 1530 it was parted in the centre, at first smoothly brushed, but after 1540 waved, before being coiled at the back under the French hood. Young girls or brides had long, flowing hair.

The gable hood, of black silk or velvet, had gaily decorated or coloured front-lappets, embroidered or jewelled (Figs. 1, 3, 5). From 1525 these were generally turned up over the hood, leaving the sides of the linen undercap curling out below (Figs. 1, 3, 4, 7). The material or curtain hanging at the back was divided into two pieces by 1525 (Figs. 1, 6), and one was sometimes folded up on top of the hood (Fig. 7). During the thirties the gable was replaced by the French hood (Fig. 9), set well back on the head, showing the hair; an English version also appeared, being similarly rounded at the top although set flatter on the head with the sides pointed (Fig. 8). These hoods had only one narrow flap or pendant at the back; the front-opening was often edged with gold or silver lace and had two decorative borders or billiments (Fig. 9). The silk, velvet, or linen undercap, often embroidered, was tied under the chin from 1525.

Purses were of leather or silks, embroidered and drawn together with strings. The pomander of goldsmiths' work, containing perfumed spices, hung from the girdle.

For nobility only, by law, deep crimson and blue velvets and gold-embroidered materials. Light tawny, orange tawny, soft reds, scarlet, murrey, black, blue, greenish blue, light and dark greens, blue-green and greys and russet colours were worn.

Side notes:
Gown and fastenings
Black-work and *cut-work*
Partlet
Lace
Petticoat
Sleeves
Separate undersleeves
Girdle and sash
Hair
Gable hood
French hood
Gold or silver lace
Billiments
Undercap
Purses and *pomanders*
Colours

73

Edward VI – Mary (1547–58)

1556

middle-class
1558

2

1553

3

4

5

1547–53

apprentice
or serving-man

18

EDWARD VI—MARY (1547–58)

Men's Fashions

SPAIN influenced fashions, and knitting was introduced from the Continent.
The fitting doublet was high-necked with a small standing collar (Fig. 5); **Doublet**
front fastenings were buttons and buttonholes or loops; or crochets and loops *Hooks and*
(hooks and eyes) were used, being hidden, giving an edge-to-edge join (Fig. 5). The *eyes*
doublet sometimes had a double skirt, giving a fuller effect; sleeves were fitting but with **Sleeves**
a shoulder emphasis; as from *c.* 1545 a stiffened 'wing' was added at the armhole (Fig. 4, *Wing*
also on gowns Figs. 1, 3). Doublets of velvet, satin, canvas, etc. often differed from
breeches or jerkin, and were occasionally 'pinked' (p. 91, Fig. 3) or slashed (Fig. 4). *Pinking*

The gathered edging or narrow ruffle of linen at the top of the neckband of the shirt *Ruffled frill*
(Figs. 4, 5) later, from *c.* 1560, developed into the ruff. This neckband sometimes had a
small turned-down collar or 'falling band' (Fig. 3). *Falling band*

The jerkin, put on over the doublet, was similar in cut, although when the front **Jerkin**
of the doublet was padded and stiffened at the end of this period, the jerkin was not. It
was made often without sleeves, or it had sleeves with the front seam left open, so
that they could hang free from the shoulder, or it had a short full sleeve with long,
hanging or false sleeves; velvet, satin, woollen cloths, frieze, or felt were used, and, *Leather or*
from *c.* 1550, leather, often plain at first (Fig. 4), later shaped and fitting as doublet. *buff*

Leg-coverings remained as before; middle and lower classes generally had the full, **Hose**
pouched upper part (breeches or trunks) longer, almost to the knee, with the long,
tailored hose sewn to them, of cloth cut on the cross (Figs. 4, 5).

Cod-pieces were gradually discarded, no longer being used after 1570. **Cod-pieces**

Knitted stockings of silk or wool were first mentioned in 1553; short ones, or **Stockings or**
'nether stocks' of thick yellow wool became common later, for working-men and youths *nether stocks*
(Fig. 3); the boys of Christ's Hospital, founded by Edward VI, still wear yellow stockings
and long blue coats today. Knitting at this time was commonly done by men and women; **Knitting**
previously, from the late fifteenth century, imported knitted caps and gloves had been
for nobility only; after 1560 knitting became an important craft, and many knitted *Monmouth*
garments were worn. Caps were knitted in Monmouth in 1548. *cap*

Broad-toed shoes were proclaimed no longer fashionable during Mary's reign. **Shoes**

Gowns, always worn out of doors by any man of taste, were generally long **Gowns**
(Figs. 1, 5), but some young men preferred them short, or, very occasionally, a short
cloak instead. The sleeves of the gown were generally short and full to the elbow **Cloaks**
(Figs. 1, 5); long sleeves were still worn by the middle class (Fig. 2). Serving-men
and apprentices wore thick, dark-blue cloth coats (Fig. 3), sometimes made without
sleeves, thus showing the sleeve of the doublet. Frieze, broadcloth, etc. were used. **Hats and**

The crown of the hat was slightly fuller and the brim was flat. The soft cap was worn **caps**
by older men. Apprentices wore knitted caps. Colours on p. 77. **Colours**

Edward VI — Mary (1547-58)

1558
1

middle-
class
1558

2

3

4

5

1553-58

EDWARD VI—MARY (1547-58)

Women's Fashions

SPANISH fashions made their appearance in England with the introduction of the farthingale. Steel needles replaced the drawn-wire ones about 1555-58, resulting in an increase in fine embroidery, cut-work, and lace. *Steel needles*

The well-fitting bodice became more low-waisted when the farthingale was worn (Fig. 5) and the neckline was high, with the stiff, lace-bordered or linen collar supported on a fine wire frame (Figs. 1, 3, 5). *Gown* / *Lace*

The full skirt was fashionable until *c.* 1545, when an underskirt after the Spanish fashion, called the farthingale, was introduced (Fig. 5). This was a petticoat that had a series of hoops, smaller at the top, sewn up it at intervals (Plate IV). Earlier in the sixteenth century Spanish women had stiffened their skirts with hoops of rushes or cane, so that the large, beautifully patterned brocades, damasks, velvets, and silks showed to greater advantage. This foundation spread the skirt outwards to the hem, showing the rich petticoat or 'forepart' at the front opening; the back of this petticoat was often made of inferior material. Long aprons were seen more, as part of ordinary dress (Plate IV). *Spanish farthingale* / *Forepart*, or petticoat / Aprons

Sleeves became more fitting, and either they finished at the elbow with cuff and under-sleeves (Fig. 5) or they were long to the wrist, sometimes with the upper part accentuated (Figs. 1, 3), or with wings added (Fig. 5); the tabbed borders round the armhole (Fig. 3) or neck were called 'pickadils'. Gowns were of damask, brocade, velvet, silks, satin, fine, soft woollen cloths; also fustian and woollen cloths and russets were used. Fastenings were at side or back. *Sleeves* / *Pickadils*

The loose over-gown was similar to those worn by the men. Hanging full from the shoulder, it was open in front, sometimes fastening at the throat. Fur linings were fairly usual (Fig. 4); sleeves were long, puffed at the shoulder. *Overgown*

The waved hair, with centre parting, was visible at the front of the hood. *Hair*

Throughout this period the French hood was worn, although the top was more flattened (Fig. 5), often being dipped in the centre (Figs. 3, 4). From 1530 to 1615 the hanging piece at the back was sometimes turned up, the end projecting over the forehead; this 'bongrace' protected the face from the sun. From 1520 to the 1580's a small white fur cap, a 'Lettice' cap, was worn out of doors at times (Plate IV); and from the mid-sixteenth century small muffs were carried, often being suspended from the girdle, like the decorative pomander (Figs. 3, 5). *Hoods* / *Bongrace* / *Lettice cap* / *Muffs*

Straight pins were used a great deal to secure and fasten many items. *Pins*

Velvet shoes were popular; silk and leather were also used; they were heelless. *Shoes*

Deep red, scarlet, soft reds, purple and black, also greens, blues, tawny, and russets were worn. Watchet (light greenish blue) was favoured in Edward's reign, and a light grey-blue was worn from 1553. Dark blue, the colour of the apprentice or serving-man's coat, was the mark of servitude in the sixteenth century; it was thus in Roman times. *Colours*

77

19

ELIZABETH I (1558–1603)

Men's Fashions

THE outstanding features of Elizabeth's reign were the huge goffered ruffs, the doublet with the 'peasecod belly', and the short trunk-hose. Foreign weavers, encouraged to settle in England, introduced many fine new materials that were softer and more glossy than any used before.

Ruff
Setting-sticks
and steel
'pokers'
Starch
Cartwheel ruff

The goffered frill, or ruff, attached to the neckband of the shirt was of quite moderate proportions at first (Figs. 2, 4); of fine cambrics or lawn, it was often lace-edged, or all of lace from *c.* 1570 (Fig. 9). The setting-sticks of bone, ivory, or wood were replaced after *c.* 1573 by steel 'poking-sticks', which gave much finer goffering. After 1564, when starch was introduced into England from the Continent, ruffs reached enormous proportions, particularly in 1580–*c.* 1610, with the 'cartwheel' ruff (Figs. 1, 3); smaller or medium-sized ones were worn by 1600—some men wore this size throughout (Plate IV). By the seventies most ruffs were separate from the shirt, being tied with band strings (tasselled ties). From *c.* 1590 to 1620 ruffs were made of two or more layers (Fig. 7). Although coloured starches were talked of, white was most usual.

Band strings

Falling band

Worn from the 1540's, the falling band or collar was used for over 120 years; being small at first, it became wider later; usually of linen, it was often lace-edged from the seventies (Figs. 8, 12, and Plate IV) or embroidered in coloured silks and metal thread, from the forties to the seventies and on, in black-work, which was also used to embroider men's shirts at neck and wrist.

Black-work

Doublet
Peasecod belly
Hooks and
eyes
Sleeves

The doublet, worn under the jerkin, developed a low pointed waist, which by 1580 was padded out, forming the 'peasecod belly' (Figs. 3, 6). The buttons down the front were often false, the fastening being at the side, by means of hooks and eyes, as on a doublet in the London Museum of *c.* 1570. The skirt of the doublet, made in overlapping flaps, concealed the points which fastened hose to doublet. The sleeves, often full and stiffened at the shoulder, either matched (Fig. 3) or were separate detachable ones (Fig. 6), being fastened on at the armhole by points or buttons, which were hidden by the wings; these stiffened welts accentuated the shoulders from *c.* 1545 to 1640. Doublets were of taffeta, satin, velvet, or brocade; also fustian and canvas were used; slashing and pinking was fashionable (Fig. 9); the doublet was often different material from the other garments. A velvet of two colours, tuft-taffeta, was worn from 1570.

Wings

Tuft-taffeta
Jerkin

The jerkin, worn over the doublet, was cut similar, but was made without the front padding, and it frequently had no sleeves (Fig. 1), or it had short ones or hanging sleeves, or false hanging sleeves. The leather jerkin of 1545–75 often had the front cut into narrow strips or 'panes', or it could be pinked, slashed, and paned as well.

Panes
Mandilion

From 1577 a short, loose jacket, or mandilion, was worn, having the side seams left open; it was put on like a cloak, with the sleeves hanging front and back; it was worn by soldiers and gentlemen until *c.* 1620.

78

Elizabeth I (1558~1603)

1

2

3

4

5

6

1580

1602

7

8

9

10

11
1580

12

Trunk-hose	The upper part of the leg-covering was now called the trunk-hose; the part covering
Bombasted	the hips being puffed and padded out with horsehair, bran, or cotton-wool; also they
	were usually made in wide strips or panes, showing the linings (Figs. 1, 2, 6); the panes
	could be braid-trimmed, slashed, or pinked and were usually of a different material
	from the doublet (Plate IV). During the eighties trunk-hose were often very short
Venetian hose	(Fig. 1), contrasting with the long Venetian hose which were introduced *c.* 1570 and
Whole hose	were very fashionable (Fig. 3). The garment consisting of breeches and long stockings
Stockings	sewn together was termed 'whole hose' or just 'hose'. 'Stockings' applied to the shorter
	separate ones worn with Venetian hose or looser style of breeches (Figs. 11, 12, and
	Plate IV); also to the short stockings gartered below the knee (Fig. 6 and Plate IV),
Canions	over a separate upper part, known as canions, which were sewn to the trunk-hose.
Knitted	Stockings were tailored, from material cut on the cross, until *c.* 1600, when knitted ones
stockings	of silk, worsted, or thread replaced them; the clocks were often embroidered.
Breeched	Small boys still wore petticoats until about six years old, when they were 'breeched',
	a practice which lasted well into the late eighteenth century. Breeches were loose, of
	knee-length (Plate IV).
Shoes	The shoes, of fine Spanish leather, silks, brocade, velvet, cloth, also other leathers,
Wedge heel	remained heelless until nearly 1600, when a wedge of leather or cork was inserted under
	the heel (p. 85, Fig. 9*a*), or an extra piece was added (Fig. 6).
Gown	Long gowns, with either short sleeves (Fig. 5) or only a winged sleeve (Fig. 11),
	were worn; also by the end of the reign, gowns with hanging sleeves were common
	(p. 85, Fig. 6). Collars and facings were of velvet or fur (fox or wolf).
Cloaks	The short flared, nearly circular cloak was extremely fashionable from *c.* 1545 to
	1620 (Figs. 2, 3). It usually had a standing collar and was richly trimmed. Cloaks were
	of velvets or silks to match the doublet or trunk-hose, or were of frieze or woollen
	cloths.
Hair	For most of the reign the hair was short (Figs. 4, 11), but longer hair covering the
	ears became more usual by the nineties (Figs. 3, 6).
Beards	Neatly pointed beards, usually fairly short, were fashionable for most of this period,
	but longer, bushy beards were seen for a short while about the 1580's.
Bonnets	Small flat hats, or 'bonnets', continued in fashion until 1570, when they were usually
	worn by the lower classes, but a small type was worn at Court during the eighties (Fig. 1).
Hats	The soft-crowned Spanish hat (Fig. 4) and the stiff-crowned hat (Fig. 2) were favourites,
	of silks, taffeta, or velvet and, later, felt. High-crowned beaver hats were worn from
	c. 1560 (Figs. 8, 9, 10, and Plate IV). Flat caps and caps or bonnets of knitted wool were
Caps	worn by apprentices. The round embroidered indoor cap or 'night-cap' was rarely
Colours	seen out of doors except on the elderly (Fig. 7). Colours are shown on the women's
	page (p. 83).

ELIZABETH I (1558–1603)

Women's Fashions

RUFFS and the French farthingale dominated women's dress; whole gowns were often embroidered, and new and elaborate materials were worn by the wealthy. Women's ruffs were similar to those as given on the men's page, being small at first, attached to the neck of the smock (Figs. 1, 9), with separate ruffs usually from the 1560's to the 1630's, both these forms being often left open in front from 1555 to 1570. Blue and white starches were used, and the lace edging and lace ruffs were exquisite (Plate IV). Falling bands or collars were not yet usual on women. For ceremonial occasions unmarried women wore high fan-shaped ruffs, wired up behind the head, leaving the bosom bare (Fig. 6) usually from 1570 to 1625. From 1580 to 1635 a stiffly wired 'plain' collar, or rebato, was worn; at this time the silk-bound wire supports, or 'under-proppers', for collars or ruffs were often called 'pickadils' (Plate IV).

Ruffs

Fan-shaped ruff
Rebato
Under-proppers
Pickadils

The gown was usually open in front, showing the stomacher, the top of the smock (or chemise), and the petticoat or forepart (Figs. 3, 8, 9). More often after 1545 the bodice, or 'body', was made separate from the skirt, being stiffened inside with 'stays' or 'busks' of wood or whalebone (Figs. 6, 10), with the full weight of the skirt hanging separate over the farthingale. With these wider skirts the bodice was often made as a doublet, being fastened at the left-side with hooks (Fig. 5).

Gown and stomacher
Separate 'body'
Stays and busks
Hooks

Sleeves fitted at the wrist, swelled out at the shoulder (Fig. 3), being stiffened or decorated with pickadils (Fig. 2) or wings (Figs. 5, 8) or puffs (Plate IV), or were puffed and padded to such an extent that any movement must have been very difficult (Fig. 6), one of the symbols of the wearer's social status. The male fashion of false or separate hanging sleeves was also adopted (Plate IV).

Sleeves

False sleeves

The wide-spreading skirt remained in favour (Fig. 8), the supporting farthingale was not always worn (Fig. 9), but from the 1580's skirts usually spread outwards from the hips, sometimes to enormous proportions. The French farthingale of the 1580's–1620's consisted of a padded roll worn round the hips under the dress (Fig. 7), with the greatest width at the back and sides, the front hanging fairly straight (p. 88, Fig. 4), the English version projected at the front as well as at the back and sides. Another type which stood out flat like a wheel round the hips, tilting slightly up at the back, was held out on silk- or cloth-covered supports of wire or whalebone (Figs. 5, 6, and Plate V); a flat form of ruff, or 'frounce', was worn over the projecting part of this style (Fig. 5); from the eighties skirts were often shorter to the ankle. Velvet, fine linen, silk, satin, taffeta, and damasks of rich quality were worn by the upper classes, with much use made of embroidery, over the whole gown (Fig. 8) or the petticoat (Fig. 10), or the bodice or sleeves (Plate IV), in coloured silks with metal thread, or entirely in black silk; fustian, fine woollen cloths, coarser cloths, serge, and russets were worn, with the wealthy merchant classes imitating nobility.

Farthingale

French and English farthingales

Wheel farthingale
Frounce

Embroidery
Black-work

81

1562
1

1587
2

1583
3

4

Elizabeth I (1558-1603)

5

6
court dress
1600

7

1580
8

1576
9

10
1580

The loose over-gown was still in use (Fig. 4, and p. 88, Fig. 5); the dainty slashed embroidered gown (Fig. 8) could also be worn straight and unbelted. They were sleeveless with wings, or with short sleeves or long hanging or false sleeves.

Knee-length tailored hose was replaced by knitted ones of silk, finest yarn, or worsted by 1600, being gartered above or below the knee with small embroidered sashes or bands. Both men and women often wore two pairs of stockings.

Shoes were made of velvet, silk, and Spanish and English leathers, and were often finely embroidered. Cork wedges were used towards the end of the reign to heighten the heel.

Hair was shown much more, with only a small cap on the back of the head (Figs. 2, 9), although the earlier styles persisted at first. By the nineties the hair was dressed off the forehead over a high pad (Figs. 5, 6). Hair-dye, false hair, and wigs were worn by the rich; pearls were popular as a decoration on formal occasions. Girls and unmarried young women wore their hair long and uncovered, even out of doors (Plate V).

The cap or coif was usually embroidered, in black-work or coloured silks; it was often worn under the hat (Fig. 4). The dainty lace cap, dipping over the forehead, was called a shadow (Fig. 10). Hoods of the earlier reign were still seen well into the eighties, particularly among country folk (Figs. 1, 3, 8). An arched hood, with the front edge wired into a wide, dipping curve, was sometimes worn out of doors or for mourning; it draped round to the shoulders or waist.

Hats followed the male fashion, becoming much more common by 1600 (Fig. 4).

Long ropes of pearls or gold chains were worn (Figs. 5, 6, and Plate IV), with jewels and costly trinkets, for both sexes. Small mirrors and purses hung from the girdle.

Feather fans were fashionable (Plate IV); the folding fan appeared *c.* 1590 (Fig. 6).

Oval or half masks were worn to hide the face from the sun, or from public gaze; they were of various colours—*e.g.*, green, grey, brown, or black—and made of velvet, silks, or satin, lined with thin silk.

From 1570 small muffs were fashionable (Fig. 4 and Plate IV), also fringed silk scarves (Plate V), worn round the neck above the ruff or collar.

Yellow, orange, tawny, straw colour (1578), bright tan (fashionable for the Queen and nobility), peach, flame and rose colours, soft reds, scarlet and crimson, purple-reds, black (more for men), blues, watchet, greens and sea-green (a changing colour), cold and warm greys, white and russets. Elaborately embroidered gowns or suits in rich natural colours, or all in black-work on white linen, were very popular among the wealthy.

Marginal notes:
Overgown

Hose or
  stockings
Garters
Shoes

Hair

False hair
  and *wigs*

Caps
Shadow
Hoods
Arched hood

Hats
Jewellery

Fans
Masks

Muffs and
  scarves
Colours

20

JAMES I (1603–25)

Men's Fashions

THOUGH the ruff, peasecod belly, and short trunk-hose began to go out of fashion during this reign, they were retained for State functions. Longer, loosely gathered breeches, long boots of fine, soft leather, and the falling ruff were some of the main items of fashion for everyday wear.

Neckwear
Standing band

The ruff continued for some years (Figs. 2, 6), also the plain or lace-edged falling band (Fig. 1), but from c. 1605 to 1630 a standing band or collar (Fig. 4), often made of transparent material and lace-edged, became quite popular, being held out round the throat on an 'under-propper'. From 1615 the falling ruff was seen a great deal; it was made of two or three layers of fine linen or lawn (Figs. 3, 5) and often lace-edged. It was gathered in to a deep band round the neck and tied with tasselled band strings.

Falling ruff

Doublet

The neck of the doublet was made with a high standing collar round the throat (Plate V), and the deep neckband of the falling ruff was worn inside it, so that the ruff sloped downward on to the shoulders. The front of the doublet was still deeply pointed and stiffened, even boned (Fig. 5), but the exaggerated padding of the peasecod belly was discontinued. The deeply pointed, tabbed skirt of the doublet was sometimes decorated with bows or ribbons with tag ends (Fig. 5), being the points which secured the breeches to the doublet; these were visible only when the eyelet holes were made in the waistline above the tabs, otherwise they were concealed underneath them, when a belt or sash was worn round the waist (Figs. 2, 3, and Plate V). The doublet was lined and sometimes quilted inside, and usually front-fastened with buttons. The sleeves became more fitting, with fairly wide wings round the armhole, and at the wrist small linen ruffles were worn with the ruff, or a turned-back cuff with the standing band or falling ruff (Fig. 3). The doublet and breeches were now usually made to match, velvets, satin, and fustian being used a great deal, also taffeta and silk damask, canvas and cloth; braid trimmings were fashionable.

Points

Quilted
Sleeves

Jerkin
Leather
jerkin

The jerkin was still used until c. 1620–30, when a sleeveless leather one became popular (Fig. 1); it was of military origin. It was usually made without sleeves, or it had fabric ones sewn in under the wings, thus doing away with the necessity of wearing a doublet.

Breeches

Trunk-hose with short canions were the most usual, being made looser and generally more bulky than the Elizabethan style; the stockings were usually pulled up over the canions and tied with sash garters (Plate V). Other types of breeches were a well-padded or 'bombasted' form of Venetian hose (Fig. 2); an unpadded type fastening below the knee (Fig. 6); and 'Dutch' breeches, 1600–10 (Fig. 7). Loose, bulky breeches generally became much more usual (Figs. 3, 5), some being decorated with ribbon points and trimmed at the side with braid or buttons (Fig. 5); these were popular between 1620 and the 1630's.

Venetians
'Dutch'
breeches

84

James 1 (1603-25)

1
1611

2

3

4

5

6

1605

7

8   9   a

b

Stockings	Knitted stockings were much more generally used, reaching usually above the knee, and were of silk and very costly, or of worsted, thread, or wool; two or even three pairs were worn in cold weather. Stockings were coloured—e.g., red, green, or grey. Tailored stockings continued in use for some years yet, being of woollen cloth or wool mixtures, silk, satin, fustian, worsted, or kersey. Sometimes part of the stocking was tailored and the visible part knit.
Sash garters	Small sashes with fringed ends gartered the stockings below or, usually, above the knee (Fig. 3 and Plate V).
Boot-hose	Thick overstockings, worn inside the boot and called 'boot-hose', now had the tops lace-edged, making them decorative leg-wear, and not merely functional, as previously (Fig. 8).
Boots	Riding-boots with spurs (Fig. 5) were fashionable for walking from 1610, and continued so for fifty years. They were made of fine, soft leathers and were usually close-fitting, reaching well above the knee when fully pulled up; more often the tops were folded down, showing the coloured lining, which could be of velvet or satin. A well-wrinkled boot showed that the finest, softest leather was used.
Shoes Rose	The round-toed shoes were at first tied with quite a small bow (Fig. 2) or small rosette (Fig. 3 and Plate V); this after 1610 became a huge rose (Fig. 9*b*), being for display, concealing the tie underneath. Shoes were usually of leather, which was often waxed. Cork was used to heighten the heel, at first as a wedge (Fig. 9*a*), which was still seen until *c*. 1620, but more usually small heels of wood or leather were worn (Fig. 9*b* and Plate V); sometimes the leather sole continued under the small block heel, as at p. 88, Fig. 1.
Red heels	The heels and the sides of the soles were coloured red for full dress; this remained in fashion for Court wear until late in the eighteenth century.
Gowns Cloaks	Long gowns of damask or cloth were seen only on elderly men; the sleeves, often braid-trimmed, were slit in front, so that they hung from the winged shoulder. Cloaks were of varying lengths and were extremely fashionable, knee-length ones being the most popular (Fig. 5); they usually matched the doublet and breeches, or the lining matched, or velvet was used.
Hair	The hair was longer, covering the ears; small beards and moustaches were worn.
Hats	High-crowned hats of various shapes and sizes were of beaver or felt; brims of the larger hats were 'cocked' in various ways. Hats were worn indoors, even for meals up to 1680, and in church to 1660, but not in the presence of the King.
Gloves	Gloves were much more commonly used (Fig. 5), even perfumed ones, but gauntlets finely embroidered and fringed (p. 88, Fig. 6) were most fashionable.
Rapiers	Rapiers were still worn (Fig. 3 and Plates IV, V), but not daggers after 1605.
Colours	Colours are given on p. 89.

JAMES I (1603-25)

Women's Fashions

STIFF foundations and padding remained in fashion until 1615, when skirts hung gracefully from a new high waistline, and ruffs were discarded.

The closed ruffs of medium to large size continued at first (Figs. 1, 3, 5), and were sometimes seen as late as *c.* 1630 on elderly women; the fan-shaped ruff was rarely seen after 1615 (Fig. 4), but a wide oval ruff was fashionable for married women from *c.* 1625 to 1650, and a falling ruff, as worn by the men, appeared *c.* 1615 (Fig. 6) and lasted until *c.* 1630. The plain lawn, lace, or cambric collar, the rebato, also continued in use until *c.* 1630 (Fig. 2 and Plates IV, V), being held up underneath by the tabbed and stiffened support or pickadil; the tagged ends of the band strings tying the collar can be seen under the pickadil and collar of the young woman's doublet in Plate IV. A plain or lace-edged falling collar or whisk appeared about 1623 (Plate V). Ruff

The bodice of the gown continued long and straight, still sloping forward at first to a deeply pointed front; either it was a separate garment from the skirt (Figs. 2, 4, 5), perhaps as a stiffly boned doublet (Plate V), or as a boned and busked upper part of the dress (Figs. 1, 3), the front being either low-necked or high round the throat; the false front was either buttoned, tied with bows, or was hooked at the side; from the 1620's fastenings were at front or back, of laces, hooks and eyes, or small jewelled clasps.

Fashionable unmarried women often had the neckline low and square at first (Fig. 4), but from 1605 to 1625 very deep U-shaped styles were popular (Fig. 6), some examples even exposing the whole bosom.

From 1615 the waistline, though still pointed, rose to a new high level (Fig. 6 and Plate V), with the skirt sewn to it, or the bodice part still retained the features of the male doublet, plain, braid-trimmed, or fully embroidered.

For the first twelve to fifteen years the skirt continued to be supported on the French (Figs. 4, 5), English (Fig. 3), or wheel farthingales (Figs. 1, 2), the frill or flounce hiding the hard edge of the wire or whalebone foundation (Figs. 1, 4, 5), or sometimes a reversed flounce was used (Fig. 2). The forepart of the petticoat at the front opening was usually beautifully embroidered, or it was of a much richer material than the gown. From 1615 fashionable women discarded these cumbersome foundations, and skirts hung straight from waist to hem (Fig. 6).

Long sleeves, some still puffed and padded at the shoulder, were worn with the farthingale (Figs. 1, 4); they were still decorated round the armhole with the tabbed border or early pickadils (Figs. 3, 5), or with the wings.(Figs. 2, 6), which were seen from *c.* 1545 to the 1640's. Sham hanging sleeves continued to be worn at first (Plate V), but these disappeared with the new full shorter sleeves of 1615 (Fig. 6), which were often slashed down the front, showing the sleeve of the smock (chemise).

Finely embroidered gowns, bodices, and petticoats—*i.e.*, foreparts—were very

87

Marginal glosses (right column): Ruff; Oval ruff; Falling ruff; Rebato; Pickadil; Band strings; Whisk; Gown; Bodice; Fastenings; Skirt and farthingale; Forepart; Sleeves; Wings; Hanging sleeves

James I (1603-25)

1618   1

2

1612   4

1616   5

3
1605

1615   6

fashionable among the wealthy (Plate V), usually linen being used. Later satin was popular, also damask and soft silks, perhaps lined with velvet for extra warmth; also various woollen and linen cloths were worn.

The over-gown hanging open in front, and falling full from the shoulders (Fig. 5), was rarely seen after 1620. Usually it was made with no sleeves, but it retained the wings; sometimes it had wings with long, hanging, false sleeves. Velvet, fustian, woollen cloths, and braid trimmings were used. Over-gown

The hair was still dressed over a roll in front (Figs. 1, 3), sometimes being puffed high in the centre (Fig. 4 and Plate V). With the advent of the new, more graceful fashions the caps were no longer worn, and the hair was brushed back from the forehead and coiled in a 'bun' on the back of the head with the sides loosely curled and fluffed (Fig. 6). Ribbons, jewels, and even ostrich feathers decorated the hair on special occasions. Hair

Small hoods and caps were still worn with the earlier form of hairdressing (Figs. 1, 3, 4), with long veils being usual for widows (Fig. 2). The embroidered linen cap or coif was worn under the tall, crowned hats (Fig. 5), which followed the male fashions. The sugarloaf hat was one most frequently seen, with the popular twisted crêpe band (Fig. 5); this was common for married woman and countrywomen. Caps
Hats
Sugarloaf

Silk-, worsted-, or thread-knitted stockings were replacing the tailored cloth or woollen ones; they were of various colours. Stockings

Heels of most shoes, which were similar to men's, were now raised with cork or shoes had cork soles; ribbon bows and ties were small (Fig. 1, 3). Shoes and *cork heels* and *soles*

The apron, worn by housewives for centuries, had now become a very fashionable accessory; it may have served as an attractive protective covering for the elaborate and beautifully embroidered forepart, as it was usually of a transparent silk or gauze, trimmed with lace, embroidery, or fine cut-work. Plain white aprons were also worn, of linen or holland. Aprons

Scarves and small muffs were used in the winter, and the folding fan was carried (Fig. 3), also the earlier form of feather fan, which continued in use until the eighteenth century. Gloves were beautifully embroidered (Fig. 6); whole, oval-shaped, and half masks continued also until the mid-eighteenth century. Scarves and fans and muffs
Gloves and masks

Since the 1590's small black patches of silk or velvet were stuck on the face with mastic, being considered an aid to beauty (Fig. 6). *Patches*

Flame and rose colours remained fashionable, also orange, purple-red, grey, greenish blue, light and dark greens, and white. Men also wore black, black and white, scarlet, deep mauve, and purple. White was usually the ground colour for the elaborately embroidered garments. Colours

21

CHARLES I (1625–49)

Men's Fashions

ACE collars, long hair, and tall boots were the chief items affected by the man of fashion. The character of the doublet and breeches changed during the thirties.

Neck-linen By 1630 the falling ruff (Fig. 3) was replaced by the falling band, which spread out over the shoulders from the high neck of the doublet (Figs. 1, 4). Smaller linen *Collars* collars, sometimes lace-edged, were also quite general (Figs. 2, 5, 6). Coloured starches were not used. Note the tasselled band strings of Figs. 2, 6.

Doublet Until 1633 the doublet was tight-fitting and small-waisted, with a deeply pointed skirt cut in overlapping flaps (Fig. 3). It was still adorned at the waist with ribbons (*i.e.*, 'points'), and at the armhole with wide shoulder-pieces. The front and back of the doublet were often slashed (Fig. 4). Later the doublet was made looser, though still well tailored (Figs. 1, 2, 4); the pointed front disappeared, and though the shoulder-pieces remained, they were much smaller. The collar of the doublet was narrow and upright round the throat. The front was sometimes left half unbuttoned at the waist, showing the shirt (Figs. 2, 4).

Sleeves At first the upper part of the sleeve was generally paned, or cut into strips (Figs. 3, 4). Later the sleeves were made fitting, sometimes with a slit in the front, and were turned back in a small cuff at the wrist, where the fine lace-edged shirt was visible (Fig. 1). Satin was most fashionable; silks, linens, and woollen cloths were also used. Sometimes an entire suit was pinked (Fig. 3) or finely slashed.

Breeches The breeches, now hooked to the doublet at the waist, were not so full, and gradually became quite tight-fitting. They at first finished above the knee (Fig. 3), later below, where they were gartered and decorated with huge bows (Fig. 4), ribbons, or points (Fig. 3), or rich cords (Fig. 2). Towards the forties, breeches sometimes left loose at the *Spanish* knee (Fig. 2), and often braid-trimmed, were called Spanish breeches.

Hose Silk stockings were the fashionable wear; more than one pair was worn in the winter. **and clocks** Since the sixteenth century a triangular insertion was made at the ankle (Plate V).

Boot-hose The lace-edged boot-hose of fine linen were used as before (Fig. 1).

Shoes For full dress shoes had red heels and huge roses in the front (Fig. 4); after 1635 wide bows were worn instead.

Boots Boots were very much used, of fine, soft leather, well fitting with fairly small turned-down tops at first (Figs. 1, 3), which became very wide later. Note the square toes again, also the flat sole added to the boots during the thirties (Fig. 1).

Cloaks Short cloaks were much favoured (Figs. 2, 4). Elderly men wore them long as in Fig. 6; and gowns with hanging sleeves continued as before (p. 85, Fig. 6). Satin or cloth was used. Cloaks were lined and were usually circular in cut.

Hats The wide-brimmed hat of felt, beaver, or even velvet, with the ostrich plume,

Charles 1 (1625-49)

1635
1

1639
2

1627
3

4

5

1642
6

middle-class

was most popular. The brim was cocked at side or front (Fig. 5); more severe flat-brimmed hats were also worn (Fig. 4).

Hair   Until 1628 the hair was level with the chin (Fig. 3), then it was curled and long to the shoulders. Moustaches and small pointed beards were fashionable; during the middle years of the reign a small tuft under the lower lip was often seen instead of the beard (Fig. 4).

Lovelock   From 1590 to the 1650's a single curled or waved tress of hair, often tied with a bow, was brought forward casually on to the shoulders; this was affected by men, sometimes also by women.

Rapiers   Rapiers continued to be worn until 1650.

Handker-   Large pocket 'handerkerchers' of cambric or lawn were carried in the hand or chiefs tucked into the slash of a sleeve. They were a decorative accessory and were usually trimmed with lace, or cut-work, or embroidery.

Gloves   Embroidered gauntlet gloves were worn by the upper classes.

Colours   Colours are shown on the women's page of this reign (p. 94).

Charles I (1625-49)

1628

1

2

3

4 middle-class

5

6

CHARLES I (1625–49)

Women's Fashions

Gown

PARIS still had a strong influence on English fashions. Some of the stiffness and paddings disappeared, and women's dresses became more graceful again.

Gown The high-waisted gown with the full gathered skirt that was worn in the latter part of James I's reign continued almost unchanged until the thirties.

Stomacher The bodice with the pointed stomacher was still worn, but was almost concealed under the gown (Fig. 1). From 1630 a skirted bodice was in favour, the skirt part being divided into six or eight pieces similar to the male doublet (Figs. 2, 3). During the first ten years skirts were open in the front, showing the elaborate petticoat (Fig. 1); elderly and middle-class women retained this fashion throughout the period (Fig. 4). The neckline was extremely low and rounded at first (Fig. 1), but was later square or V-shaped (Figs. 2, 3, 6, and Plate V).

Collar or whisk Falling ruffs were being replaced by lace or linen collars wired out at the back during the first year or two (Fig. 1), but the low spreading collar or whisk became popular (Plate V). The male fashion of wearing this collar was adopted for outdoor use (Fig. 3), and the middle class wore a similar type made of linen (Fig. 6).

Sleeves Among the upper classes the sleeves were very full and puffed to just below the elbow (Figs. 2, 3, 6); and until 1630 they were sometimes paned (cut into strips) and tied round with ribbons (Fig. 1). Frilled lace or linen cuffs adorning the sleeves were essential, and the under-sleeves were often also visible (Figs. 2, 6). Satin gowns were most fashionable. Silk and taffeta were also worn, and linens and woollen cloths for the poor.

Hair The more natural manner of dressing the hair that was introduced in the preceding reign was now very common; the side-pieces gradually became longer, hanging in soft ringlets (Fig. 3), and the fringe was often carefully arranged in flat curls.

Hats The wide, plumed Cavalier hat, made of velvet, was used for riding only (Fig. 3).
Veils Women usually left the hair uncovered, though out of doors small light veils were
Caps sometimes draped over the head and face; also lace or linen caps were not uncommon (Figs. 1, 4). Married women and country women wore tall-crowned black hats (Plate V).

Gloves During the latter half of the reign long, tight gloves that reached almost to the
Muffs elbow were worn with the shorter sleeves (Fig. 2). Muffs were usual during the winter;
Fans fans, masks (for out of doors), and small round patches on the face were quite common
Patches among the upper classes. Jewellery was not so lavishly used, but pearls remained in favour.

Colours Amber-yellow and blue were popular. Reds, scarlet, pale purple-red, white, and black (very usual for men) were also worn. Golden brown and red-browns were almost as popular as black for men. They also wore fawn, grey, dark blue-brown, dark red, blue, and green. Embroidered garments were seen at first.

94

22

THE COMMONWEALTH (1649–60)

Men's Fashions

PURITAN dress was generally more subdued than that of the Royalists, although on occasion garments of brilliant colours, richly decorated with braid or lace, were not at all uncommon. Buff coats, wide-topped, stiff leather boots, and 'Puritan' hats were characteristic of the Commonwealth.

Although the longer type of doublet was still seen (Figs. 2, 3), the fashionable style was in the form of a short jacket that barely reached to the waist (Fig. 5). It was sometimes made with the 'skirt' as only a small tabbed border; the skirt of the longer type of doublet usually had only a single slit at the back. The shoulder-pieces, or wings (Fig. 5), were fast disappearing, and the term 'doublet' fell into disuse after 1670. The sleeves were either plain, and buttoned at the wrist, or were slit in the front, displaying the shirt (Fig. 5). *Doublet*

Sleeves

Cloth was used a great deal, with silk tissue and velvet as well, with braid or lace trimmings or sometimes ornamental buttons.

The linen falling band, or collar, was frequently made to meet edge-to-edge in front from 1640 to 1670 (Figs. 1, 2), with the corners sometimes rounded after 1660 (Fig. 4). Lace-bordered collars were seen on fashionable men. *Collars*

The fine linen shirt was now an important item, for not only were the sleeves visible at the wrist or front slashing (Figs. 1, 4, 5), but the shirt itself was puffed out at the waist, filling the gap between jacket and breeches (Fig. 5). *Shirt*

Buff coats or jerkins became very common (Figs. 1, 4); they were frequently tied at the waist with a wide sash. Separate sleeves were often sewn into the armholes, and were decorated with braid or lace stripes (Fig. 4). *Buff-coats*

The belt at the waist (Fig. 4) was replaced by a wide 'shoulder-belt' for carrying the sword (Fig. 5, and p. 100, Fig. 5); it was worn from c. 1630 to 1700. *Shoulder-belt and sword*

The plain closed breeches, fastening just below the knee, continued for some years (Fig. 3); these were hooked to metal rings sewn under the skirt of the doublet. A wide, looser style, or 'open breeches', similar to wide 'shorts', became very popular and were worn from 1640 to c. 1670 (Fig. 5); they were a revival of the earlier Dutch breeches (p. 84), being cut to fit to the hips, without support other than perhaps a strap and buckle at the back; the linings of these breeches were full and gathered into a band at the knee. The ribbon- or braid-trimmed Spanish breeches were still seen for a few years (Figs. 1, 2); they were hooked to the doublet. Cloth was used for breeches unless they were made to match the doublet. *Breeches* *'Open breeches'* *Spanish breeches*

Stockings were gartered at the knee as before; lace-edged boot-hose were unchanged (Fig. 5), but after 1655 they were sometimes worn with shoes as a loose over-stocking (p. 100, Fig. 5). *Hose* *Boot-hose*

Boots remained in favour for street wear, although the tops became very wide, *Boots*

95

merchant
1657
2

The Commonwealth (1649-60)

1   3   4   5

appearing most cumbersome (Figs. 1, 5); a much stiffer leather was used. After 1660 heels, still very square, were made higher, and an even harder, stiffer leather made these jackboots suitable only for riding. *Jackboots*

Shoes of black leather had square toes and comparatively high square heels, which were still painted red for full dress. Shoes were fastened by small 'roses' or flat ribbon bows (Figs. 2, 3). Shoes

Long gowns were worn only by elderly men as formal attire (Fig. 2), and by the learned professions, or they were used by State officials. Gowns

Cloaks of varying lengths were still popular, but they were usually worn straight, hanging from both shoulders (Figs. 1, 3), and were of thick cloth. Cloaks

Beaver was the most expensive material for hats, which were generally high-crowned and had brims of various widths, sometimes being cocked, as the wearer fancied (Fig. 1). Felt was used a great deal, also a rough, hairy material called 'shag', often of worsted, or silk was used, or hair; these were coloured blue, scarlet, black, or buff. Hats were occasionally decorated with plumes or ribbons. Men continued to wear hats indoors even at meal-time, but usually after *c.* 1660 only men of superior position continued to do this. Small round caps were worn only by elderly men indoors (Fig. 2). Hats *Shag*

Hair was generally long, almost to the shoulders. The extremists had the head close-cropped; hence the name 'Roundhead' was later applied to them. Hair

Black was worn a great deal, also grey; fawn, pinkish red, scarlet, deep red, and blues were the more popular colours. Colours

The Commonwealth (1649–60)

merchant's wife 1657 1

2

3

middle-class 4

5

6

riding-habit

7

8

1656

THE COMMONWEALTH (1649–60)

Women's Fashions

S MALL linen caps and wide collars were most common. Women adopted the tall-crowned Puritan hat for everyday wear.

The gown with the full skirt and fitting bodice was little changed, though the latter tended to be more stiffly corseted and was often laced at the back (Fig. 7). The pointed waist showed signs of returning. The gown was frequently caught up, showing the petticoat (Fig. 3), and the open skirt was still worn (Fig. 1). *Gown*

Puffed sleeves continued to be fashionable, and during the first few years they were often short to above the elbow, with the full linen under-sleeve showing below, as in Fig. 6. During this period the sleeves were set in, very low off the shoulder, as in Figs. 3 and 7, and small shoulder-pieces at the armholes were still occasionally seen (Fig. 7). The deep, square-cut neck was often replaced by a fairly low, wide neckline, which revealed the shoulders (Fig. 7). Narrow lace edgings were usual with this type of bodice. *Sleeves*

Wide linen collars, sometimes with a lace border, were usual for all classes. Satin gowns were most fashionable among the ladies of rank or rich middle class; fine and coarse cloths were used. Hems were often lace- or braid-trimmed. *Collars*

Soft scarves were sometimes draped across the shoulders when low-necked dresses were worn. *Scarves*

The hair was still coiled up on the back of the head (Figs. 3, 7); the side-curls were often quite long down to the shoulders. Fringes began to go out of fashion. Narrow, coloured ribbons were worn in the hair a great deal. *Hair*

Women of all classes wore the high-crowned Puritan hat (Figs. 4, 6), plumes generally decorating the hats of the more wealthy women. *Hats*

Loose hoods of cloth or velvet, tied under the chin, were made with or without a shoulder cape (Fig. 1), and fur muffs became larger by the forties (Fig. 1). *Pug hood* *Muffs*

Small caps of linen, or sometimes lace, were seen a great deal throughout this period (Figs. 2, 5); they were frequently worn under the hat or hood (Plate V.) *Caps*

Aprons, worn by middle- and lower-class women, were long and narrow, reaching nearly to the hem of the gown (Fig. 2, and p. 102, Fig. 3). *Aprons*

Stockings reached to above or below the knee; the garters were like small sashes, buckled or tied. *Stockings*

Shoes were similar to those worn by men, with square toes and small heels, though daintier shoes were usual with the more elegant dresses (Fig. 8). *Shoes*

Dove-grey, amber-yellow, blues, white, fawn, violet, and black were popular colours. *Colours*

1680
1

1666
2

Charles II (1660-85)

3

1660
4

1666
5

6

23

CHARLES II (1660–85)

Men's Fashions

GREAT changes occurred in men's garments during the same years as the Plague and Great Fire of London. The doublet appeared for the last time.

The short form of jacket, or doublet, was seen until 1670 (Figs. 3, 4), and ribbon trimmings were still used a great deal until this date. *Doublet*

The King himself set a new fashion, in October 1666, of wearing a long-sleeved waistcoat, or 'vest', which reached at first to the hips, later to just above the knee (Fig. 1). Also new was a loose coat, thigh-length at first (Fig. 5), but it was then made fitting to the waist, hanging longer to the knee (Figs. 1, 2, 6), with a slit up to the hips at the back (Fig. 5), and later at the sides as well (Fig. 6), with the openings decorated with buttons. It fastened down the front with buttons either to the hem or to the waist only. The pockets were placed very low (Figs. 1, 2) and were at times vertical (Plate V); these 'long' pockets and the others were edged with buttons and buttonholes. Both coat and vest were collarless; sashes were sometimes worn round the coat (Fig. 1, 2). *Vest and coat* *Long pockets*

Coat-sleeves were elbow-length at first, with the longer vest-sleeve, turned up over it, forming a cuff (Fig. 2). Later the coat-sleeve had a cuff of different material, thus doing away with the vest-sleeve, or the entire vest (Fig. 6). By 1680 sleeves with small cuffs reached to the wrist (Fig. 1). Silks, satin, brocade, and woollen cloths were used. *Sleeves*

Linen or lace-bordered collars were deeper than before (Figs. 3, 4); but in 1666 they were replaced by a linen strip, tied in a bow at the throat, called the 'neckcloth', or 'cravat' (Fig. 6). The bow part could be of coloured ribbon and was called 'cravat-strings' (Fig. 2). Later the neckcloth was looped at the throat, as in Fig. 1. *Neckwear* *Cravat and cravat-strings*

The loose breeches widened still further, to 'petticoat breeches' (Figs. 3, 4, 5), but after 1666 were soon replaced by full breeches gathered into a band at the knee (Figs. 1, 2, 6, and Plate V). The great loops of ribbons decorating the outer side of breeches or garters were most fashionable, being called 'fancies' (Figs. 3, 4, 5, 6). *Petticoat breeches* *Breeches* *Fancies*

The stockings were gartered up under the knee or breeches, with ribbon or lace decoration. Boot-hose, some lace-edged and of very fine quality, were often worn with shoes (Fig. 5); sometimes they hung more loosely round calf or ankle. *Stockings and boot-hose*

Flat, wide bows or, later, small buckles decorated the square-toed shoes; the tongues became much higher. Red heels were worn with full dress. *Shoes*

After 1660 boots were used for riding only, and they were of very stiff leather. *Boots*

Cloaks were used during the early sixties (Fig. 3); but were later kept for travelling. *Cloaks*

The huge French periwig quickly became fashionable; made up of a long, curling mass of hair, it hung down front and back over the shoulders (Figs. 2, 3, 4, 6, and Plate V). Hats had low crowns (Fig. 2), the wide brim flat, or cocked, sometimes at the back only; this 'Monmouth cock' was still seen on country squires in 1711. Small round caps with a turned-up fur brim were used indoors or for travelling (Fig. 1). *Wigs* *Hats and the Monmouth cock*

Charles II (1660-85)

1

2

3

4
1660

5

1671

6

CHARLES II (1660–85)

Women's Fashions

WOMEN'S dress became more elaborate. Puritan hats and linen collars were no longer worn by the lady of fashion. Gowns were stiffly corseted down to the hips, and necklines were wide, low, and rounded.

The skirt of the gown was gathered to the bodice and either hung full to the ground (Figs. 5, 6) or it was open in the front and fastened back with ribbons or clasps, showing the petticoat (Fig. 4), or it was caught up, as in Fig. 2. The stiff bodice with the small waist now reached to the hips, and the front was pointed again (Figs. 4, 5, 6 and Plate V). Low necks baring the shoulders remained in fashion, and they were generally softened with a narrow lace frilling (Figs. 2, 6) or filmy drapery (Figs. 4, 5). The wide Puritan collars were now worn only by elderly or middle-class women (Fig. 3). _Gown_

During the first twenty years the sleeves were usually full and puffed to the elbow; later they were more loose-fitting (Fig. 2). For full dress very short little puffed sleeves were fashionable, with fine under-sleeves reaching to the elbow (Figs. 5, 6). The under-sleeves with the frilled cuffs were seen with all types of dresses. Both the puffed and longer sleeves were sometimes slashed (Fig. 2). Silk and especially satin and richly patterned fabrics were worn a great deal by the more wealthy women (Plate V). _Sleeves_

The side-curls continued in favour, and often longer ringlets were brought forward over the shoulder (Fig. 6). The hair at the back was coiled up as before, and narrow hair ribbons were still used. Very wide hair styles were fashionable; false hair or tow was probably used to give extra width. _Hair_

The wide-brimmed hats were very similar to those worn by the men, and they were used for riding only; otherwise women's hair was uncovered, except when the small velvet or cloth hoods were worn (see p. 98, Fig. 1), or the linen cap which was retained by the older women (Fig. 3). _Hats_

Brightly coloured stockings were fashionable, of silk, or wool for poorer classes; two pairs were often worn at the same time. Tailored stockings of cloth such as worsted were still in use for rough work. _Stockings_

Shoes had a more feminine character; the heels were higher and more slender, and the toes were pointed, though still square at the tips. The tongues of the shoes became much higher (Fig. 1). Brocades, satins, leather, and embroidered materials were used. _Shoes_

Small black patches on the face came into fashion again, and they remained in favour until nearly the end of the eighteenth century. _Patches_

Blues, golden yellows, white, browns, and pinkish reds were much worn. Men favoured black, browns, dove-grey, blues, and reds. _Colours_

James II (1685-89)

1688
1

1685
2

24

JAMES II (1685–89)

Men's Fashions

THE long coat had come to stay, and it was cut similar to the frock-coat; the wig was essential for every man who could afford it.

The coat was longer, to below the knee, and the skirts were full, being now pleated at the sides and back (Figs. 1, 2). Most of the buttons down the front were false, and the coat either hung open or it was buttoned only at the hips, as in Fig. 1. The slit pockets were set very low as before, and were decorated on either side with braid and buttons; the vertical, or 'long', pockets were seen up to *c*. 1715. *(Coat / Long pockets)*

The fairly fitting sleeves were generally long and turned up above the wrist in a deep cuff, showing the sleeve of the waistcoat (Fig. 1), or a false sleeve (see p. 101). Shorter sleeves, to the elbow, were still occasionally seen (Fig. 2). The lace-edged linen shirt-sleeves, falling in soft ruffles over the hand, remained in fashion until nearly the end of the eighteenth century. *(Sleeves)*

The waistcoat was longer, to the knee, and was buttoned down the front (Figs. 1, 2). Silk, brocade, satin, and woollen cloths were used as before for coat and waistcoat. Handerchiefs dangled from the pocket or were carried in the hand. *(Waistcoat / Handkerchiefs)*

The cravat, or linen neckcloth, was wider, with the ends looped over; these were often tasselled or lace-bordered (Fig. 1). *(Cravat)*

The full breeches were unchanged, and reached to below the knee. Black velvet ones were popular; they were cut to fit the hips and were buckled or laced at the back. *(Breeches)*

Stockings were gartered at the knee, with the tops rolled back, concealing the plain buckled garter. Various reds, grey, green, white, and black stockings were usual. *(Stockings)*

The square-toed shoes remained in fashion; the tongues were very tall, and small bows or buckles decorated the shoes. Red-heeled shoes were worn with full dress. *(Shoes)*

For riding, etc., boots of soft leather were used, buckled or buttoned to fit the leg. *(Boots)*

Loose overcoats replaced the cloak after 1670, although it was still occasionally used for travelling. *(Overcoats)*

The large curls of the periwig were more formally arranged, falling in ringlets over the shoulders and down the back. The ends of the shorter wigs, which were used by soldiers or travellers, were generally tied together on the nape of the neck. The head was closely cropped, and caps were worn indoors when wigs were removed. *(Wigs)*

Small caps and the hat with the wide brim often cocked at the sides were used as before. It was no longer considered correct to wear hats in the house. *(Hats)*

Swords were still seen with civil dress. Tall cane walking-sticks were often carried. *(Swords)*

The bunches of ribbons that were so popular had now disappeared, except for a small knot of ribbons that was sometimes worn on the right shoulder until 1700. Thereafter loops of ribbon or cord were worn by serving-men only. *(Ribbons)*

Colours were the same as before (p. 101). *(Colours)*

James II (1685-89)

1688
2

JAMES II (1685–89)

Women's Fashions

WOMEN'S hair was dressed differently. The bodice became even stiffer and straighter in the front, with a higher neck. Puff sleeves went out of fashion.

The gown still had a very full skirt, which was generally open in the front, showing **Gown** the shorter petticoat (Fig. 2); the sides were sometimes caught together at the back, as in Fig. 1. The bodice was made very straight and small-waisted, and the stiffened stomacher with the round-shaped ends finishing just below the girdle was fairly common **Stomacher** (Figs. 1, 2—see also stomachers in Figs. 1, 4, p. 93). The neck was made higher, covering the shoulders, and was often V-shaped (Fig. 2).

The sleeves were looser and gathered into the armhole, and were longer for general **Sleeves** use (Fig. 1), but for more formal occasions they were turned back above the elbow in a wide cuff (Fig. 2); the short puffed sleeve (p. 102, Fig. 6) continued to be worn for full dress. The under-sleeves that showed beneath the sleeves of the gown remained unchanged (Fig. 2). Silks, satin, brocade, woollen and linen cloths were used.

The hair was longer, with ringlets hanging down the back and over the shoulders. **Hair** The side-pieces were shorter and arranged in tight curls high on the head above the ears (Fig. 2). Ribbons were quite often used, and sometimes a little lace, to decorate the hair on top of the head; this developed into the very tall headdress so fashionable in the following reign.

The small hood or 'kerchief' of cloth or velvet were the most usual head-coverings. **Head-** They were worn over a small linen undercap that had the front edge slightly frilled **coverings** (Fig. 1).

Women's shoes were the same as in the preceding reign (Fig. 2). Slippers, which **Shoes** were similar to the 'mules' of today, came into fashion.

Lace or silken mittens were worn in the summer instead of the long kid gloves. **Gloves, etc.** Muffs were used a great deal in the winter. *Mittens*

The colours were little changed (see p. 103). The petticoat seen in front of the gown **Colours** was usually of a richer colour or material than the gown itself.

William III (1689 – 1702)

1

2

25

WILLIAM III (1689–1702)

Men's Fashions

HUGE cuffs, very full-skirted coats, and closer-fitting breeches were the main new features of men's garments during the last few years of the seventeenth century.

The coat was worn unbuttoned, and it hung open down to below the knee; the pleats on either side were made much bigger, making the skirt stand out full from the fitting waist (Figs. 1, 2). The sleeves were looser, with very large cuffs turned back from the wrist up to the elbow, where they were buttoned back to the sleeve (Fig. 1). The frilled lace or linen shirt-sleeve showed below the coat-sleeve as before.

The pockets were no longer mere slits, as pocket-flaps were introduced (Figs. 1, 2).

The waistcoat was shorter than the coat, reaching to above the knee, and it was left unbuttoned from the waist down. The sleeves (if any) were no longer visible. The materials used were the same as before.

The lace or linen neckbands remained unaltered.

By 1690 the breeches were cut to fit the leg, though they were still fairly full at the waistband. They were either made to match the coat or waistcoat or were of black velvet.

The stockings were gartered at the knee, but the tops were occasionally pulled up above the knee over the fitting breeches (Fig. 2).

The shoes had square toes, large square tongues, and small buckles (Fig. 1).

The lighter, more closely fitting type of boot continued, and separate leather leggings were also worn with shoes for riding. The large spur-leathers concealed the join with the shoe, so that they appeared very like boots.

Wigs were carefully curled and dressed high on either side of the centre parting, with the long ringlets, as before (Fig. 1). Wigs were not always worn by everyone, especially if the owner had a good crop of naturally curly hair (Fig. 2).

The hat had a rounded crown and a wide brim; this was turned up, or cocked, on one or both sides (Fig. 1), or sometimes on both sides and the back as well, this being the first sign of the triangular cocked hat. The edge of the brim was usually decorated with braid or gold or silver lace.

Colours were generally quiet and subdued, but waistcoats were usually more colourful than the coats. Red linings were usual for the high tongues of the shoes (Fig. 2); the tops were turned back to show the colour.

Marginal notes: Coat · Sleeves · *Pocket-flaps* · Waistcoat · Cravat · Breeches · Stockings · Shoes · Boots and *leggings* or *spatter-dashes* · Wigs · Hats · Colours

William III (1689-1702)

1693
1

2

1689
3

4
1690

WILLIAM III (1689–1702)

Women's Fashions

THE high headdress and the introduction of the bustle were new fashion features. The fitting bodice was usually open in front, with the edges turned back to show the richly patterned lining (Fig. 3); braid trimmings were used as a decoration and as part of the front fastening of the bodice at times (Fig. 2). The skirt was still caught back and up, and, to emphasize this back drapery, a small pad, or 'bustle', was worn underneath (Fig. 1), a fashion which became very popular and lasted until 1711. The skirts were long, often trailing on the ground at the back. The shorter petticoat, now fully displayed at front and sides and forming part of the dress, was often of a more elaborate material (Fig. 3) or horizontally trimmed with braid, lace, or quilting (Figs. 1, 2). *Gown* *Bustle*

One or sometimes two quilted petticoats were worn underneath for extra warmth from early in the eighteenth century, being an undergarment, not yet part of the dress. *Quilted under-petticoat*

Satin and silks were used for the dresses, also damask; striped silk linings were fashionable; linens and woollen cloths were also used.

The sleeves were no longer so fully gathered at the armhole, although they were fairly loose-fitting, with a turned-back cuff above the elbow. The fine linen chemise sleeve showing below had one or more deep ruffled frills, plain or lace-edged (Figs. 1, 2, 3), several frills being usual for full dress (Fig. 4). *Sleeves*

Only the hair waved and curled up from the forehead was visible in front of the high headdress. After 1700 the hair was sometimes powdered. *Hair* *Powder*

The ribbons and lace that decorated the hair in the previous reign were now elaborated into the headdress so fashionable for the next fifteen years or so. It was made up of a small cap on the back of the head (Fig. 1 and see 1616 style in Plate IV), with one or more folds of linen or lace and ribbon, wired up in front, with the long ends hanging from the back brought forward over the shoulders (Figs. 1, 2, 4); this erection was called the 'Fontange', and the wire support the 'commode'. *Headdress, or 'head'* *Fontange and commode*

The hood was now the general head-covering for out of doors (Fig. 3). It was worn at the back of the head, over the cap-shape, with the towering headdress standing up in the front. *Hoods*

Wide, richly embroidered scarves, hanging to the waist, were draped round the shoulders, and worn until about 1775. Muffs were very common in the winter (Fig. 3), also long kid gloves (Fig. 4) and mittens were very fashionable. *Scarves, etc.* *Mittens*

Cloaks were still worn by women in cold weather. *Cloaks*

Small aprons of rich-coloured materials came into fashion. They had frilled or lace edging, and were often beautifully embroidered (Fig. 1). *Aprons*

Orange, yellow, blues, soft browns, and reds were still worn. *Colours*

III

Anne – George I (1702–1727)

1

2

3

4

1714-27

5

6

26

ANNE—GEORGE I (1702–27)

Men's Fashions

THE three-cornered hat was now fashionable, otherwise men's garments were little altered.

The general cut of the coat was unchanged. The skirt was very full and   Coat
sometimes stiffened in the front. The side-pleats remained as before, but the pocket-flaps were made bigger (Fig. 4). The coat was usually left open in the front. The cuffs were still very large, with the lace or fine linen frills showing below. Both coat and waistcoat were still collarless. Satin, figured silk, silk and wool, or woollen cloths were used for coats, also velvet.

Pockets were made with straight flaps until about 1710, when a scalloped or curved   Pocket-flaps
shape appeared.

The waistcoat was still shorter than the coat, and the waist was closely fitting, being   Waistcoat
tightened at the back with tapes. It was usually left unbuttoned from waist to hem (Fig. 3). Embroidered satin waistcoats were fashionable.

The neckcloth, or band, plain or lace-edged, was worn either long or short (Figs.   Cravat
3, 4).

Breeches fitted the leg well to below the knee (Figs. 1, 2). They were made to match   Breeches
coat or waistcoat as a rule, or dark cloth was sometimes used.

Stockings were either gartered below the knee or, as some fashionable men   Stockings
preferred, they were pulled up over the breeches to above the knee as before (Figs. 3, 4). Black or coloured silk stockings were fashionable; woollen ones were worn by poorer men.

The toes of the shoes were inclined to be more rounded, and the tall square tongues   Shoes
were gradually going out of fashion. Buckles, square or oblong, were small up to c. 1730.

The popularity of the huge, curled periwig began to fade at the end of this period,   Wigs
though it was retained for Court functions until the end of George II's reign. The shorter wig with the ends tied back was still worn on horseback. During the twenties the long front ends of the periwig were often tied up, as in Fig. 6, with the back hair twisted into one long ringlet. This later developed into the long pigtail, or plait, worn at the back of the smaller wig.

The three-cornered hat (Fig. 5) became the only fashionable form of headwear.   Hats
With the high wigs it was often carried (Fig. 4). This type of hat remained popular for fifty years. It was of black beaver trimmed with braid or gold or silver lace.

Green, red, yellow, fawns, cool browns, dark brown, blue, and black were worn.   Colours

Anne — George I (1702-1727)

1705
1

1720
2

1720
3

1702-14
4

5

1702-14   6

ANNE—GEORGE I (1702–27)

Women's Fashions

THE old farthingale was revived in 1711 and renamed the 'hooped' skirt. High headdresses gradually disappeared, and powdered hair was seen from 1715. The 'saque', known in France during the previous century, was introduced *c.* 1720. There was an air of casualness in dress, with display of chemise, at bosom and sleeve.

The looped-back dress with the bustle remained fashionable until 1711 (Fig. 1); then the skirt was supported on an under-petticoat which had cane or bone hoops sewn to it at intervals, similar to the old farthingale, but this shape was domed (Fig. 4), and it became very popular. The neckline was low, with the bodice sometimes open in front, showing the stomacher (Figs. 3, 5, 6), with linen, lace, or muslin frilling softening the neck opening. *Gown* *Hooped skirt* Stomacher

The small puffed or paned sleeves were seen only on Court dress in Anne's reign (Fig. 4); plain sleeves with turned-back cuffs were generally worn. The falling fan-shaped cuffs on the sleeve of the early saque (Figs. 2, 3) were more usual later. Frilled muslin or lace-edged chemise sleeves showed at the elbow. Sleeves

A loose gown or sack (saque), worn by countrywomen in the late sixteenth century, was later in the seventeenth century considered fashionable in France, when a few were seen in England, but not generally accepted. About 1720 this gown, hanging loose front and back (Figs. 2, 3), was sometimes seen here, being usually of plain material; it was worn with the hooped petticoat (p. 120, Fig. 1). Embroidered panels and petticoats were found early in the eighteenth century. Gowns were of damask, silk, satin, fine woollen cloths, and linen with lace or braid trimmings. *Saque*

Men's fashions were copied for riding, hat, coat, waistcoat, and cravat. Riding-habit

At first the hair was closely curled on top of the head, with long ringlets hanging from the back (Figs. 4, 5). This fashion remained in vogue for Court wear (Fig. 2). The hair was generally done up on top of the head, as in Figs. 3, 6. Powdered hair was beginning to become fashionable from 1715. Hair

The high headdress (Fig. 1) gradually became smaller during Anne's reign (Fig. 6), until it was a mere frilled cap on top of the head (Figs. 2, 3). The two long ends hanging at the back were, however, retained for some time (Figs. 3, 6, see also p. 110). Headdress

Hoods and long wide scarves remained in use (Fig. 1). Very tiny muffs were popular 1710 to 1711. Hoods, etc.

Aprons were still worn and were longer and made of satin or other rich silks. Aprons

Women still wore cloaks in bad weather. Cloth was generally used. Cloaks

Blues, yellow, dove-grey, reds, dark green, or black were worn; cherry colour was very fashionable in 1712 for women's hoods; scarlet cloaks were quite common. Lace (of silver), brocade trimmings, and fringes were used. Colours

27

GEORGE II (1727–60)

Men's Fashions

SMALL wigs replaced the huge periwig, the stock replaced the cravat, and the very full-skirted coat went out of fashion by 1760.

Coat   During the greater part of this period the skirt of the coat was very full to the knees, being open at back and sides, with deep side-pleating (Fig. 8); the front was stiffened at first, until the coat was made narrower during the forties and fifties (Fig. 9). The coat was well 'waisted', and until *c.* 1735 buttons were sewn from neck to hem, or to the waist only from 1720 on; it was, like the waistcoat, collarless, although flat *Pocket-flaps* collars were sometimes seen (Fig. 1). Coat, waistcoat, and breeches were often of matching material, cloth being used for day wear, silk, satin, or velvet for evening or full dress (Plate VI), when they could be embroidered or decorated with lace or braid trimming (Figs. 4, 5). In 1740 cuffs and coat linings were often of a contrasting colour to the coat (Fig. 8); velvet was very fashionable for coats, also figured and corded silks and woollen cloths.

The 'frock'   From 1730 a plain coat with turned-down flat collar and no lapels, as worn by working-men, was increasingly used for informal wear. It was looser in cut, fastened usually with metal buttons, and was called the 'frock'; it was not braided, trimmed, or embroidered and need not match waistcoat or breeches.

Sleeves   Coat-sleeves barely reached the wrist, so that the frilled sleeve of the shirt was well displayed (Figs. 8, 9). Cuffs were very large during the thirties (Fig. 4, 5); some reached *Boot cuffs* to the elbows and were called 'boot' cuffs. Also during the thirties and on to 1750 some cuffs were made with a slit on the outer side, some sleeves had no cuffs at all, but had a buttoned side-slit; but cuffs generally became smaller with the more fitting coat (Fig. 9).

Waistcoat   The waistcoat, like the coat, was at first stiffened in front, and was long nearly to the knees (Fig. 5), and usually made with sleeves until *c.* 1750. It was often richly decorated, and it became shorter from the forties (Plate VI).

Neckcloth   The loosely tied neckcloth, or cravat, was still seen until the forties, usually on *Stock* elderly or poorer men; but from 1735 a stiff, folded neckband called the stock, fastening round the throat at the back, became very fashionable (Figs. 4, 5, 6, 9); the ruffled edge of the shirt-front could thus be seen at the open front of the waistcoat.

Necktie or   The ribbon ends of the black bow on the wig were sometimes draped over the *solitaire* shoulders and fastened with a brooch at the throat, or they were tied round the throat, fastening in a bow at the front (Figs. 1, 4), appearing like an early form of necktie. This 'solitaire' was seen from the 1730's to the 1770's.

Breeches   Breeches matching the coat, or of velvet, silk, or cloth, were cut low to fit round the hips as before, and were buttoned and buckled at the knee (Plate VI); they were usually made much more fitting, although remained full in the seat.

116

George II (1727-60)

1   2   3   4   5   6

8

7   1740-45   9

Stockings	Stockings were still rolled up over the knee at first until *c.* 1750, but from 1730 it became more fashionable to buckle the breeches over the stockings (Figs. 5, 6).
Shoes	At first shoes still had high square tongues, square 'high' heels, and blocked, fairly square toes, but these became rounded from 1740, with lower heels and small tongues, with small square or oval metal buckles until *c.* 1730, when they tended to become larger.
Boots	Boots with bucket tops were for riding only. They were sometimes cut down and shaped to the back of the knee; also black leather leggings, buttoned on the outer side, were worn with shoes when riding.
Banyan	An Indian nightgown or banyan, a long, knee-length loose coat or négligé, was frequently worn indoors for relaxing, when the wig was also laid aside, and a pouched velvet 'nightcap' put on over the shaven head. By the early nineteenth century, the banyan was ankle-length, more in the form of an elegant dressing-gown.
Nightcap	
Overcoats	Thick cloth overcoats, loose in cut, but similar to the coat, had one or more large collars; the top one could be turned up and buttoned over the chin, and the large cuffs unbuttoned and folded down to cover the hands (Fig. 7).
Wigs	Men of all classes wore wigs, the large periwig being retained by older men for some time (Fig. 5); smaller wigs were generally used by young men by 1730. The front and sides were fluffed out into curls (Fig. 8), which were later arranged in neat rows; the top was shaped up in the centre without a middle parting in the thirties, and by the fifties this front was raised higher (Fig. 2). The long, hanging ends of the smaller wig were tied at the back with a black taffeta bow into a tail or 'queue' (Figs. 8, 9).
Queue-peruke	
Ramillie	When the hair was plaited into a long tail, with sometimes a bow at the bottom as well (Fig. 6), it was known as a 'ramillie'.
Bag-wig	The short tail of the queue was occasionally put into a small bag that matched the bow (Fig. 3). This bag-wig was worn indoors only at first, but it soon became popular for everyday use.
Hats	The three-cornered hat remained in favour, and was usually trimmed with lace, braid, or even a narrow feather edging (Fig. 9).
Colours	Claret colour was fashionable in 1740. Greens, blues, light and dark browns, corn colour, reds, and small patterned material (*e.g.*, of orange and crimson) were also worn.

GEORGE II (1727-60)

Women's Fashions

THE hooped skirt developed still further during this reign; plain satins and silks gave way to rich, large patterned damasks and brocades (Plate VI); the saque, or sacked-backed gown, became the height of fashion, with the French influence increasing in the fifties. Powdered hair was worn for full dress.

The neckline was low on most dresses, with either a soft frilled muslin edging (Plate VI) or a white embroidered muslin kerchief draped over the shoulders and covering the neck opening, being tucked in showing the stomacher (Fig. 3), or it was held in place with bows or ribbon ties or laces (Figs. 5, 6, 9).   *Gown* / *Neckerchief* / *Stomacher*

The sleeves were generally loose-fitting at first, with a deep, wide cuff (Figs. 1, 3, 5, 9), but during the forties the sleeve narrowed and became more fitting, with a slender winged cuff, pleated in the front, spreading out to a wider shape over the elbow from 1740 to 1750. This was replaced by the falling fan-shaped cuff (Figs. 4, 8, and Plate VI), which could be double or treble. Separate frilled muslin ruffles, lace-edged or often embroidered in white, completed the sleeve (Plate VI); these also were double or treble; otherwise the frilled chemise sleeve was seen up to about 1740 (Figs. 1, 3, 5, 6, 9).   *Sleeves* / *Winged cuff* / *Falling cuff* / *Ruffles*

The large, dome-shaped hooped petticoat (worn under dress of Fig. 1) spread sideways during the forties, the front and back falling almost straight down from the waist, spreading out fan-wise (Figs. 3, 4, 9). A smaller, bell-shaped hooped foundation was also used; but from the 1740's to the 1760's the width moved upwards on to each hip, so that the skirts were supported on a short hooped petticoat or 'side-hoops' (Fig. 8), or pocket hoops for the smaller version. Later a frame was devised that was hinged (Fig. 7), so that the sides could be lifted up, thus enabling the wearer to pass through a narrow space without walking sideways.   *Hooped petticoat* / *Fan hoop and bell hoop* / *Side-hoops and pocket-hoops* / *Hinged hoop*

A pair of pockets were tied round the waist, under the hooped foundation (Fig. 7), both the dress and petticoat having slits each side.   *Pockets*

The gown was usually closed at first (Fig. 3), but during the forties the skirts opened in front, showing the petticoat (Figs. 4, 9); this was usually embroidered or quilted, the plain lozenge quilting (p. 126, Fig. 1) being the earlier form, when this garment was part of the underwear; on petticoats that were meant to be seen the quilting was more elaborate (Fig. 4 and Plate VI).   *Quilted petticoat*

The dress that became the most fashionable during this period was the sack-backed gown, which remained popular until nearly 1780. At first the pleated back and front hung loose from the shoulders (Fig. 1); later the front and sides were moulded close to the figure, leaving the pleated back hanging in one long length from neck to hem (Fig. 8), displaying the beautiful fabric. Another robe seen from 1740 to the 1750's was a dress with a wrap-over front, having the bodice continuous with the front skirt; it was tied with a sash round the waist and was usually of silk or satin.   *Saque* / *Wrapping-gown*

119

George II (1727–60)

1730

1

2

3

1750

4

5

6

lower-class

frame for the hooped skirt

8
1760

9
1744

Plain silks and satins of the earlier years were replaced by floral patterns of large and elaborate designs (Plate VI), and figured and brocaded damasks more typical of this period, becoming lighter and more delicate towards the sixties, often with a striped pattern. Embroidered cuffs and robings (flat trimming round neck and front of bodice and skirt) were seen from the late forties and the fifties; from the fifties there was an increase in decoration with bows and ribbons, flounces and furbelows (pleated trimming); see Fig. 8 and Plate VI.

Robings

Flounces and
  furbelows

Hair was dressed close to the head, with more of an upward movement by the sixties (Fig. 8), when there was an increasing use of powder for formal occasions.

Hair

Small frilled caps were worn on top of the head, older women often having the front ends tied under the chin in the forties; this was seen on younger women in the thirties.

Caps

Small hats were worn over the linen or muslin caps (Figs. 4, 5, 9); they were decorated with flowers and ribbons, sometimes being tied round with a bow under the chin, appearing like shallow bonnets. Dark-coloured hoods with long tie-ends were worn (Fig. 2), also wraps or cloaks in cold weather.

Hats

Hoods
Wraps

White stockings were fashionable for full dress by 1740, otherwise coloured ones such as blue or green, often with embroidered clocks, were gartered at the knee.

Stockings

Shoes were made of leather or fabric, often matching the dress, being fastened on the front, with tie or buckle. Toes were very pointed at first (Fig. 9), and the sole was rounded, not being shaped for left or right feet. Heels were heavy and curved, becoming smaller and more slender during the fifties (Fig. 8). Wooden soled pattens were worn to protect shoes out of doors; the uppers were of leather or silk to match the shoes. Since *c.* 1630 the flat wooden 'sole' was often raised on an iron ring.

Shoes

Pattens

Silk garters were most usual, tied above or below the knee; by the late eighteenth century the finest ones were padded silk with tiny brass-wire springs, covered in silk, added at one end; these were then tied with ribbon.

Garters

During the earlier years long aprons were most usual (Fig. 9), of muslin or silken gauze, lace-edged, plain, or later embroidered in white. From 1730 to 1750 short ones of silk were fashionable, being richly embroidered in coloured silks (Fig. 4); later longer aprons returned to favour. This decorative accessory formed part of fashionable women's dress well into the seventies and eighties.

Aprons

Silk, cotton, or kid mittens were worn during this century.

Mittens

Light, slender fans were fashionable, usually of ivory with leaf of silk or skin; the more expensive ones were beautifully painted (Figs. 3, 8, 9).

Fans

Rose-pinks, yellows (often of a brilliant mustard colour), blues, greens, browns, and rich reds were worn, some silks having a watered effect. White with brocaded or sometimes embroidered flower sprays was very fashionable by the sixties. Quilted petticoats were also in rich and brilliant colours, although, to judge from those that survive, blue was a favourite.

Colours

28

GEORGE III (1760–1820)

Men's Fashions: PART I (1760–90)

A GREAT many changes occurred in men's fashions during the first thirty years of this reign. Wigs were discarded; hats, coats, waistcoats, and breeches were all altered. During the seventies extremely high wigs, tiny hats, and shorter fitting garments were affected by 'exquisites' called 'Macaronies'; this nickname was taken from the Macaroni Club, which was formed by very fashionable young men who had recently travelled in Italy, and who adopted eccentric fashions; it was also applied to very fashionable young women.

Macaronies

Coats lost their fullness (Fig. 3), and the front was sloped away to the sides (Figs. 1, 2, 6). The one-time side-pleats were now placed well at the back (Fig. 5). Riding-coats were sloped away in the front from neck to hem (Fig. 5). Dandies wore the coat shorter, to above the knee. The sleeves were longer and more fitting, and from 1770 the cuffs became smaller, with the ruffled frill of the shirt showing at the wrist. From 1765 the 'dress' coat was made with a narrow standing collar, which became increasingly higher (Fig. 2). From 1785 there was a style which turned over into a 'stand-fall' (Figs. 1, 6), this particular collar being a development of the earlier turned-down collar on the 'frock', a coat which became gradually more fashionable, until from *c.* 1770 it was worn for full dress, even at Court. Until 1780 the 'frock' was single-breasted (Fig. 6 and Plate VI); then it was worn double-breasted with collar and lapels (Fig. 4).

Coat
Riding-coat

Sleeves

Standing collar
Stand-fall
Frock

Embroidered coats were seen until *c.* 1780 for formal wear, with embroidered velvet, satin, or silk coats being retained for Court wear until the turn of the century. Cloth gradually replaced the use of silk for coats, and the high stand-fall collar was frequently made of velvet (Fig. 6).

Embroidered coat

Waistcoats, now generally sleeveless, were cut much shorter than the coat (Figs. 1, 2, 3), until they were waist-length by the mid-eighties and cut straight at the bottom (Fig. 6), when they were usually double-breasted, sometimes with, sometimes without, a standing collar. Embroidered satin waistcoats were most fashionable during the seventies, and stripes were popular in the eighties. Macaronies usually affected shorter waistcoats than was usual at the time (Fig. 3), and they discontinued the use of pocket-flaps.

Waistcoats

Macaronies had their fine neckcloth or stock tied in a bow at the front (Fig. 3 and Plate VI), otherwise it was unchanged, with the ruffled shirt-front, sometimes lace-edged, worn as before. The black ribbon, or solitaire, remained in use during the sixties and seventies.

Stock

Breeches were made very close-fitting and higher at the waist by the nineties, when they were held up by braces. From early in the century working-men had worn plain braces or 'gallowses', which became increasingly fashionable during the eighties. Breeches were usually of silk or cloth; striped materials were fancied by dandies (Fig. 3);

Breeches
Braces, or *gallowses*

George III (1760 – 1820)   part 1 (1760 – 90)

2   3   4   5   6

1772

1775 – 80

1786

1788

Buckskin	velvet was usual for Court wear (Fig. 2); buckskin was used, particularly for riding-
Stockinette	breeches; dark-coloured stockinette was worn before 1790 (Fig. 5).
Stockings	Lighter-coloured stockings were most usual; striped ones were sometimes seen in the late seventies.
Shoes	The leather shoes were round-toed with medium heels, with square or oval buckles.
Boots	Boots began to appear again for street wear during the eighties (Fig. 5).
Wigs	Wigs were fairly high off the forehead with rows of curls on either side (Figs. 2, 3), or they sometimes had one fat roll right round the wig, as in Figs. 4, 6. Macaronies wore extremely high wigs (Fig. 3). In 1790 the ramillie (see p. 118) often had the end of the pigtail looped up and fastened at the top (Fig. 4).
Hair	During the eighties wigs began to go out of fashion, and the hair was frequently powdered and dressed after the fashion of the day; but unpowdered hair became increasingly popular.
Hats	The three-cornered hat continued to be worn for the first fifteen to twenty years, and was cocked in quite a variety of ways. Before 1780 the front and back were often
Bicorne	turned up (Fig. 1), and so formed the 'bicorne' of Fig. 6. Small three-cornered hats were often carried by the wearers of tall wigs; or tiny hats, similar to Fig. 4, were
Beaver hat	quite common for Macaronies. Fairly tall-crowned beaver hats with wide brims, rather similar to the Puritan hat, became popular, particularly for the sporting man (Fig. 5).
Sticks, etc.	Long cane walking-sticks with elaborate tops and tassels were generally carried by the dandies during the sixties and seventies (see p. 126, Fig. 4). Swords were no longer
Muffs	worn with civil dress, except for Court wear. Muffs were sometimes carried in the late eighties or early nineties.
Colours	Crimson, blues, browns, greens, grey, and black were worn. White or light-coloured embroidered waistcoats were popular. Striped materials were used for coats and breeches. The velvets, particularly those for Court suits, were often striped, being of two or three colours, giving a very rich appearance. The embroidery on these was lavish, with metal thread and sequins used with the finely coloured silks, which showed up well against the darker colour of the velvet.

GEORGE III (1760–1820)

Women's Fashions: PART I (1760–90)

THE changes in fashion during this long reign were very marked; passing through several phases, they went from one extreme to another before George IV came to the throne, from wide, stiffly trailing robes and delicate looped-up silks to printed cottons and plain, long-sleeved dresses and transparent muslins.

During the first fifteen to twenty years the full-skirted gown supported on the hooped foundation remained open in front, displaying the petticoat, which was quilted (Fig. 1 and Plate VI), sometimes very elaborately, or it was embroidered (Fig. 4), or decorated with frills, flounces, and furbelows into the seventies (Plate VI). _Gown_

Trained robes were worn for full dress (Fig. 4), supported on wide side-hoops, a style that remained in use at Court as late as 1820. Skirts were often shorter to the ankle, particularly with the looped-up dresses of the seventies, and with the saque, when the petticoat was shorter than the robe, which trailed on the ground at the back; but longer trailing dresses tended to return in the late eighties to nineties (Figs. 6, 12, and Plate VI). _Furbelows_ _Side-hoops_ _Court dress_

Sleeves were elbow-length until the mid-seventies, with the flared hanging cuff of the fifties and the fine lace or muslin embroidered ruffles showing below as before (Figs. 1, 4, and Plate VI). Turned-up cuffs and pleated frills appeared from 1770 to 1775 (Figs. 2, 6); then sleeves lengthened to below the elbow, becoming wrist-length in the eighties (Figs. 10, 11, 12, and Plate VI). _Sleeves_

The popular saque continued on into the seventies (Fig. 4), and with the fashionable thinner silks it was sometimes used with the 'polonaise', when the skirt was looped up by means of tape-ties inside (Figs. 2, 5); this became a style typical of the seventies, and with the use of printed cottons it continued into the mid-eighties. The bodice was often made fitting at the back, with sewn-down tapering pleats, known as the English back. _Saque_ _Polonaise_ _Printed Indian cottons_ _English back_

Elaborate decoration of the dress reached its peak in the seventies, but more simple styles were usual in the eighties, with an increasing use of cottons and plainer cloths (Plate VI). Hooped petticoats were discarded, but the back gathers of the higher-waisted dresses of the eighties to nineties were held out on pads or 'cork rumps' (Figs. 6, 12, and Plate VI), which were later known as 'bustles'. _False rumps, or 'bustles'_

In the eighties the closed robe returned, the petticoat no longer being visible; and riding-coat dresses were worn (Fig. 12), also jacket, waistcoat, and skirt outfits (Figs. 10, 11). _Riding-coat dresses_

Necklines were low and square at first, showing the stomacher (Figs. 4, 5), until the bodice front closed in the seventies, meeting edge to edge. By the eighties necklines were deeply rounded, with the muslin neckerchief, puffed and draped out in front, filling the opening (Figs. 6, 7, 12, and Plate VI). _Stomacher_ _Neckerchief_

Brocaded and figured silks were fashionable at first, with plainer silks and cottons,

125

George III (1760-1820)
part 1
(1760-90)

1
1767

2
1775

3
1775-
80

4

5

6

7
1786

8
1783

9
1770

10

11

1780

1779

1790

12

and printed cottons in the eighties, followed by woollen cloths with velvet for skirt or underskirt (Fig. 12).

At first the hair was still dressed close to the head, but the top was gradually emphasized (Fig. 1), until by 1770 the hair was arranged over a high frame or pad of tow with false curls and ringlets added; powder was lavishly used; ribbons, flowers, feathers, jewellery, even model ships, etc., decorated this erection (Figs. 2, 4, 5). Once properly dressed it was said to 'keep' for three weeks! Towards 1780 the headdress tended to widen (Fig. 6), and powder was not used so much during the day. By the end of the eighties powdered hair was discarded, and the natural hair was arranged in soft turls on top of the head, with ringlets at the back (Fig. 12 and Plate VI). *Hair* *Headdress* and *wigs*

The tiny frilled caps (Fig. 1) swelled out to enormous proportions during the seventies (Fig. 3). They were often worn over the headdress during the day, and the edges were trimmed with one or more rows of pleated frills. Smaller caps were also worn which still retained the two hanging ends at the back (seen under the hats of Figs. 6, 9, see also p. 120). *Caps*

Large hats were perched on the front of the high headdress (Figs. 2, 9, 11), but when the wider fashions came in during the early eighties hats were set flat on the head (Figs. 6, 10, and Plate VI). Simple beaver hats, after the male fashion, sometimes with very wide brims (Fig. 7), were worn with the natural curling hair (Fig. 12). *Hat*

A large collapsible hood called the 'calash', made of silk over a wire frame, was worn over the high headdress (Fig. 8). Pink linings were popular. *Calash*

Patches, paint, and powder were much used in the seventies. *Patches*

Short aprons were usual during the sixties, often beautifully embroidered (Fig. 1); others were dark-coloured with a bib front; during the seventies they were longer, of embroidered muslin, or gauze trimmed with ribbon, and long, plainer aprons were worn in the eighties (Fig. 6). *Aprons*

Small muffs were carried in the seventies and eighties (Fig. 8), usually of padded silk. Wraps, shawls, and cloaks were worn, also jackets and long caped coats for riding. *Muffs, wraps and coats*

Silk, brocade, or leather shoes had more rounded toes in the sixties with slender curved heels, which decreased in size as the century progressed, although the pointed toe returned; oval or square buckles fastened the shoe over the instep. *Shoes*

Large dome-shaped umbrellas were first used *c.* the 1750's, being a rarity and too heavy for women to carry. Lighter-weight ones were in use in the eighties (Fig. 6) and small parasols were made in the late nineties. *Umbrellas* *Parasols*

A great variety of colours were worn, from soft greens and browns to rich reds and delicate pinks and blues; plum colour was popular in the seventies, but even more fashionable was a brilliant mustard-yellow. White was particularly liked until the late seventies, with floral sprays figured, embroidered, or brocaded, usually of a larger pattern at first. Striped patterns were most fashionable, sometimes with flower sprays, or with trailing floral designs on the printed cottons of the late seventies to eighties. Narrow striped patterns were much used on the lighter silks in the latter half of this period, such as green and white, or red and white, also white with pale and dark greens. Trimmings were often in the more delicate colours. *Colours*

GEORGE III (1760–1820)

Men's Fashions: PART II (1790–1820)

THE top-hat replaced the cocked hat, the cutaway, or 'tail-coat', made its appearance, and pantaloons and trousers replaced knee-breeches.

Coats
Cutaway, or
dress coat
Tail-coat

In the nineties the sloped-back sides of the 'dress' coat were curved sharply away from below the waist, as in Fig. 4. The coat was then cut square across the front, with the sides hanging straight from waist to knee (Figs. 2, 6). This new 'tail-coat' was double-breasted, with a high, turned-over collar (which was often of velvet) and turned-back lapels (Figs. 3, 4, 6). From *c.* 1803 there was a notch in the shape of an 'M'

M-cut collar in the join of the collar and lapel; this 'M'-cut collar was found on some coats for the next fifty years, but on evening coats it remained in use until *c.* 1870. The cutaway, or tail-coat, was worn buttoned up for formal day wear, but was left open for evening occasions, a fashion which persisted for evening coats into the twentieth century (p. 160, Fig. 11).

Frock-coat
From *c.* 1816 the 'frock' was usually termed 'frock-coat' when it was used for formal wear, being by then a waisted, close-fitting coat, hanging straight from neck to hem (p. 134, Fig. 1). It was usually buttoned to the waist, often being single-breasted and sometimes with a roll or 'shawl' collar; it was later made double-breasted with collar and lapels. About 1816–18 some frock-coats were worn very long, hanging to mid-calf or just below; at first they were much ridiculed.

Sleeves
Sleeves were frequently made without cuffs and were longer, often reaching to the knuckles (Fig. 4). From now on cloth was generally used for coats; embroidered satin or velvet ones were for full dress.

Waistcoat
Waistcoats were short to the hips, but they showed below the cut-away front of the coat (Figs. 2, 3, 6). They were also single- or double-breasted with revers. Striped materials were fashionable.

Neckwear
The linen stock was worn even higher round the throat (Fig. 4).

Collar
Soon after 1800 the collar of the shirt was seen above the stock, which was generally tied in a bow at the front, or a tie of coloured material was often worn (Figs. 1, 3, 6). With the stock worn so high, almost to the ears, movement of the head was rather restricted and of necessity stiff, but the manners of many young men were quite the reverse, as it was considered 'fashionable' to look slovenly and behave coarsely.

Breeches
Breeches were high at the waist and cut very tight-fitting (Figs. 2, 3); from the eighties the fastening at the knee was often ties instead of the buckle. For indoor or informal wear, and later for evening dress, knee-breeches were often replaced, by 1790,

Pantaloons
Trousers
Strapped
trousers

with ankle-length, close-fitting pantaloons, like those worn by the children (Figs. 7, 8). Also for informal wear, trousers were worn, from 1807, for out of doors; they were generally made of nankin, and either reached to the ankle (p. 134, Fig. 1) or were longer and strapped under the instep (Fig. 6); they quickly became very popular, but elderly

128

George III (1760 – 1820)   part II (1790 – 1820)

1   2   1803 3   1799 4   1790 5   6

1787 7   1799 8

or country men retained the knee-breeches for some years. In 1814 trousers that were

Cossacks   extremely wide in the leg, being pleated into the waistband, were known as 'Cossacks'; they either were gathered in and tied round at the ankle or, later, were a little less wide and were open at the bottom, reaching to just above the ankle.

Boots   Boots continued to be fashionable at first (Figs. 1, 3), and from 1800 the Hessian

Hessians   boot became most popular for street wear (Fig. 2).

Shoes   Lace-up shoes replaced the buckled shoe with the advent of the trousers.

Overcoats   Overcoats followed the fashion of the double-breasted coat, but the wide cape-like collar remained (Fig. 1). Thick cloth was used, with collar and revers of velvet.

Hair   After 1790 natural, unpowdered hair was general, and it was cut shorter and brushed carelessly forward over the forehead (Fig. 4), which added to the general air of untidy roughness which was fashionable among young men.

Hats   Though the bicorne (Fig. 3) continued to be worn, the tall-crowned beaver hat with the wide, curling brim gradually replaced it (Figs. 5, 8). During the nineteenth century the crown was made taller and slightly wider at the top, and the brim became

Top-hat   smaller, curving well up at the sides (Figs. 1, 2, 6). Thus it was that the top-hat made its appearance, and it has continued to be worn in a slightly more modified form up to the present day.

Colours   Black was very fashionable for coats, especially in the last ten years of the eighteenth century. Browns, grey, dark blue, red, and especially green were much worn, either striped or plain. Bright-coloured waistcoats were worn with the darker coats. For evening wear the coat was blue, with a white waistcoat and black breeches; the silk stockings were often striped. White breeches were still fashionable for the greater part of this period.

GEORGE III (1760–1820)

Women's Fashions: PART II (1790–1820)

URING the third part of this reign the fashionable world looked to ancient Greece for its inspiration. The waistline rose to a new high level, 1794–1820; tight bodices and stiffly boned stays were discarded, and white was the reigning 'colour' for nearly all this period. Finally bonnets and wide-skirted gowns came into fashion, and stays pinched in the waist once more.

After 1794 the waistline rose much higher, and the emphasis at the back declined, although a small pad continued to be used for some time, supporting the back gathers of the dress. With the coming of the classical (Fig. 4) or so-called Empire period, the long, clinging muslin skirts trailed on the ground at the back for day or evening wear until 1806 (Plate VII), but by 1810 the long, trained dress had disappeared. Some women dampened their petticoat or chemise (not the dress) so that the undergarment clung to the figure, leaving the dress itself free, as if clothing a sculptured form. By 1814 skirts increased in fullness and became a little shorter to the ankle, with the hem at first decorated with frills, then corded hems and ruchings, so that it swung outwards at the bottom (Figs. 6, 8, 9), a fashion that finally led up to the crinoline style nearly forty years later. The waistline reached its highest level in 1816–20, and the neckline on evening dresses was very low (Figs. 4, 6).

At first sleeves were short to the elbow (Figs. 3, 5, and Plate VII)—for evening wear they could be even shorter—or were long to the wrist, when they were often tied round with ribbons (Fig. 4, 6). Soon after 1810 long sleeves were fashionable for day wear, and from 1815 shoulders were emphasized (Fig. 7), and by 1820 sleeves were puffed at the shoulder (Fig. 9).

From the late 1790's muslin was used a great deal for day or evening wear, plain or spotted; later spot prints, often with delicately printed borders, or tiny, coloured, woven spot patterns appeared. Linens and cottons were printed with small patterns on a dark ground in 1790–1800; there were also some white cottons with small floral prints. Gauze over silk was popular for evening gowns soon after 1800, with satin from 1810 for dinner dresses, also silk or silk-and-cotton mixture for both day and evening wear.

The frilled muslin neckerchief was worn until the end of the nineties (Fig. 3); with some of the low-necked muslins and printed cottons, the frilled muslin tucker was popular, the finely pleated layers round the neck giving almost the appearance of a small ruff (Fig. 7). Plainer collars (Fig. 9) and plaid or check scarves and sashes were seen at the end of this period (Fig. 8).

After 1800 various forms of coat or frock-coat called a pelisse were worn over the muslin dress (Fig. 7); buttoning down the front, the pelisse was sometimes a little shorter than the dress. It was of silk or a woollen cloth when it was at times made with a double or treble shoulder cape, like a man's box coat. Long coats, sometimes without sleeves,

Margin notes:
Dresses

Empire

Damped muslin

Sleeves

Indian muslins

Gauze

Neckwear
Muslin tucker

Pelisse

131

George III (1760-1820)
part II (1790-1820)

1 1798
2
4 1812
5 1799
7 1815 -18
8 1814
9 182?
3 1796
6 1816

appeared in the earlier part of this period (Fig. 5). Little short coats of silk, velvet, or even muslin, called 'spencers', were worn with muslin or gauze dresses, just covering the tiny bodice; they remained in use while the waistline was high, but disappeared as waists returned to normal level during the 1820's (Fig. 9). *Coats* *Spencer*

Kashmir shawls, introduced with the Indian muslins, were much used from the late eighteenth century (Fig. 6). The rich colour and finely woven borders showed to great effect against the whiteness of the dress. Light veils covering the head and face and shoulders were seen during the first few years, and long buff gloves were worn with the short sleeves (Figs. 3, 5). White feather or fur muffs, now very large indeed, frequently had a matching tippet or stole. Cloaks of silk or woollen cloth were used in cold weather, or for travelling. *Kashmir shawls* Veils, gloves / Muffs and tippets / Cloaks

Hair was arranged in curls at the front, with a large coil or ringlets hanging at the back (Figs. 1, 3, 5, and Plate VII); later the hair was coiled up on top of the head, with short ringlets and curls at front and sides (Figs. 4, 6, 9); it was often tied with ribbons after the ancient Greek styles; wigs were used until *c.* 1810. Hair

Various shaped turbans and ostrich feathers were most fashionable with the new high-waisted dresses (Fig. 1 and Plate VII); they were still worn with evening gowns until the early 1830's (Fig. 3, p. 136, and Fig. 5, p. 140). *Turbans*

The bonnet (Fig. 2) developed from the ribbon-tied hat of the 1750's (p. 120); the crown and brim became larger by 1814 with the higher hair style (Fig. 8); it was decorated with ribbons, feathers, or scarves. The beaver type (Fig. 7) was at times flat at first and more like the feather-trimmed hat of Fig. 9. *Bonnets* / Hats

From 1780 to nearly 1800 shoes had increasingly pointed toes and ever decreasing tiny curved heels (Plate VII); by *c.* 1800 round-toed shoes with no heels at all became general (Figs. 6, 8, 9). Silk, satin, cotton, or leather was used for these heelless pumps, which remained in fashion for fifty years. Shoes / *Pumps*

Handbags, or 'reticules', made their first appearance when the clinging muslin dresses were worn, as pockets could no longer be concealed, as they had been before, under voluminous petticoats (Figs. 4, 9). Bags were of silk, often embroidered; later they were bead-embroidered. In the eighteenth century a long, knitted 'stocking' purse was used by men and women to carry money in their pockets. In the early nineteenth century these, knitted or 'netted' in silk or thread, were usually small, about seven inches long, with tasselled ends and metal slides. *Handbags*, or *reticules* / *Stocking purse*

White was most popular for day and evening dresses during most of this period, but silks in yellows, pinks, and blues, and other soft colours appeared from *c.* 1814, and coloured satin under white embroidered net or gauze was fashionable for ball gowns during 1816–30. From *c.* 1810 day dresses of white with small spot or sprig pattern in colour were seen, and from 1813 some white dresses had coloured bodices. The tiny spencer was usually dark blue and sometimes black; occasionally it was of white muslin, matching the dress, although dark colours were more usual. Colours

George IV (1820-30)

1820
1

1830
2

3

4

5

6

29

GEORGE IV (1820–30)

Men's Fashions

TOP-HATS and long trousers were accepted by all classes, and were worn well into the following century; frock- and tail-coats were equally fashionable. Elegant young men, or 'dandies', wore their clothes extremely tight, even going so far as to wear corsets.

The tail-coat remained as before, with the collar set very high at the back. For morning wear from 1825 the riding-coat, with the front sloping away at the sides (p. 123, Fig. 5), was increasingly used, but worn a little shorter than before; it was later called the 'morning coat'. The frock-coat was popular (Fig. 1), and in 1823 it was seamed at the waist. Tail-coats for evening wear were of blue cloth with gilt buttons. **Coat Morning wear Frock-coat Evening wear**

The sleeves were well fitting, and were made with or without cuffs. When cuffless they were generally longer, almost covering the palm of the hand (Fig. 2). The coats were made of cloth, and the collars were often of velvet. **Sleeves**

Waistcoats were seen a little below the cutaway coat (Fig. 2); they were usually made with revers, which could be worn showing in the front of the coat (Fig. 3), but plain waistcoats without revers were also seen (Fig. 4). Silk or cloth was used. **Waistcoat**

Collars were very high above the folded stock, which was often replaced by a tie (Fig. 4). These were sometimes very large, but smaller bow-ties with the stock were quite common (Figs. 1, 2). The frilled shirt-front (Figs. 1, 3) was now fast disappearing, and the plain shirt was visible above the waistcoat (Fig. 2). **Collars Ties**

Trousers could be short to above the ankle (Fig. 1), but the 'Cossacks' were more usual, being strapped under the instep from 1830 (Fig. 2). They were made of white nankin or similar cloth. For evening dress the fitting breeches, either of stockinette or fine cloth, knee-length, or ankle-length pantaloons, could even be flesh-coloured. **Trousers 'Cossacks'**

Though the buckled shoe was still sometimes worn, lace-up shoes or short boots laced at the side (Fig. 1) were more fashionable for day wear. **Shoes**

The Hessian boot was now used more for riding or travelling. **Boots**

Overcoats with the one or more cape-like collars remained in fashion (Fig. 6). **Overcoats**

The hair was cut close to the head, but it was by no means short. **Hair**

The side-whiskers were allowed to grow quite long. *Side-whiskers*

The chin was clean-shaven and moustaches were very occasionally worn (Fig. 4).

The crown of the top-hat was very high, and the brim was curled well up at the sides. Black, white, or fawn beaver was used, or occasionally black felt. **Top-hat**

Dark colours, such as black, blue, brown, or grey, were most usual for coats. Brightly coloured or striped waistcoats were very fashionable, or they sometimes matched the coat in colour if not in material. For day wear at first, colours were often quite brilliant for waistcoats and even trousers, which could be of canary yellow. It became usual for trousers to be lighter in colour than the coat. **Colours**

George IV (1820-30)

1820
-23

1

1822
-25

2

1827-28

3

1826-28

4

1830

5

GEORGE IV (1820–30)

Women's Fashions

VERY full sleeves, delicate gauzes, and large bonnets became the main features of fashion; after 1820 the waistline fell and skirts increased in fullness.

Although the waistline was still fairly high at first on both day and evening wear (Figs. 1, 2), it gradually fell, until by 1828 the tightly corseted waist was almost to normal level, a fashion that spread to all classes. The deeply pointed neckline or V-shaped trimming in the bodice helped with the illusion of the downward trend (Figs. 1, 3, 4, 5). The neckline, square at first, became rounded, then 'V'-shaped, but remained very wide. *Dresses*

The frilled muslin collars or tuckers were still worn at first, but as the shoulders widened, embroidered muslin pelerines or collars spread out from the neckline, particularly from 1828 to 1833, with the long front ends tucked under the belt. *Collars and pelerines*

The skirt was at first gored and smoothly fitting at front and sides, with the centre back very fully gathered (Figs. 1, 2); later it was gathered all the way round (Figs. 3, 5); the gauze of Fig. 4 is so gathered, but the silk under-dress is smoothly fitting. From c. 1823 to 1828 the hems of silk or gauze dresses were often padded, and the decoration round the hem increased, making the skirt swing outward. *Skirts / Padded hems*

Until 1825 the tiny decorated puff sleeves were fashionable for evening wear (Figs. 1, 2), then long sleeves, very fully gathered at the shoulder, tapering to a fitting cuff, became fashionable for day or evening wear (Figs. 3, 4, 5). *Sleeves / Gigot sleeve*

Day dresses were of printed cottons, silk, or fine cloth; silk or silk-damask dinner gowns were usual, with silk net or gauze over silk or satin for evenings. Fine woollen cloths trimmed with satin, or muslin over glazed cambric, were also worn. From 1822 seams in muslin dresses were piped, a fashion which became usual on most dresses later, especially during 1840–70. *Piped seams*

Silk cloaks, colourful shawls, and delicate scarves were popular (Fig. 5), and large white feather muffs and long matching stoles were seen at first. *Cloaks / Shawls, muffs*

A centre parting with ringlets and curls worn high on the head was the typical hair style; for dances younger women wore flowers and ribbons; feather-decorated turbans were for older women, and frilled muslin caps were worn indoors. *Hair / Turbans*

Straw and even beaver bonnets became very large, with trimmings of feathers and ribbons; huge, filmy hats were worn at dinner parties (p. 140, Fig. 1). *Bonnets and hats*

Heelless shoes, or 'pumps', had rounded toes, but these became square-shaped by the thirties; they were usually of satin, white for evening and black for day; cloth and leather were also used; they were not shaped for left or right feet. *Pumps*

White or soft colours that toned well together were most popular; patterned materials—e.g., of blue and brown—or flowered dresses were worn for day with prints of a more flowing design; white, pink, blues, blue-grey, lilac, soft green, and pale yellows, rich strong yellows, reds and blues were also seen. *Colours*

William IV (1830-37)

1831
1

1837
2

1834
3

riding-habit

30

WILLIAM IV (1830–37)

Men's Fashions

THERE were no outstanding changes in men's fashions during these few years, except for the adoption of the glossy silk hat in place of the dull-surfaced beaver. When the silk hat was first worn in London by its inventor, John Hetherington, in 1797, it created a riot, and it was said that he had tried to "frighten timid people".

The frock-coat, straight in front from neck to hem, was most usual (Fig. 3), though the cutaway type was still seen at first (Fig. 1). It was tailored to a small waist as before, and was long to the knee until nearly the end of the reign, when slightly shorter coats were more correct. The back-pleats and collars remained as before. Coats for riding in town had cutaway fronts and curved tails (Fig. 1).

The sleeves were inclined to be fuller at the shoulder, otherwise they were unaltered. The cutaway coat remained fashionable for evening wear. Cloth coats were general.

Waistcoats were shorter by 1835 (Fig. 3), and the pointed front was much favoured. Brightly coloured or striped materials were still used.

The collar was high, and the wide, folded stock or tie was often brightly coloured, spotted, or striped (Figs. 2, 3); occasionally the collar was turned down, as in Fig. 3. The white stock with the bow-tie was also worn (Fig. 1), and the plain shirt-front was seen above the waistcoat.

The trousers were fairly fitting to the leg and were strapped under the instep. Between 1834 and 1836 they were sometimes made full at the waist, as in Fig. 3. The shorter fitting trousers or pantaloons (similar to Fig. 8, p. 129) remained in vogue for evening wear until about 1840. White nankin, grey, and black cloth trousers were worn.

Fashionable men often had quite pointed toes to their shoes (Fig. 3).

The overcoat was double-breasted, and towards the end of the reign the front was sometimes trimmed with braid (Fig. 2). The waist was small, and the coat was shorter above the knee by 1837.

Hair fashions were unchanged; side-whiskers were still in favour (Figs. 1, 3), and moustaches and occasionally short beards as well were worn.

The crown of the top-hat was very tall and slender during most of the reign, and the brim was small (Figs. 1, 3). By 1837 the crown became lower and wider with a slightly larger brim (Fig. 2). Beaver hats were still worn, but the silk ones became increasingly popular, and they eventually replaced the earlier type from c. 1830 on.

Black was much worn, and also blue, grey, and browns as before. Black or blue coats were correct for evening wear, with black fitting trousers.

Frock-coat
Cutaway
coat
Riding-coat

Sleeves

Waistcoat

Neckwear

Trousers

Shoes
Overcoats

Hair

Top-hat

Silk hat

Colours

William IV (1830-37)

dinner dress
1

1837
2

3

1830
4

1834
5

6
183

ball dress

WILLIAM IV (1830–37)

Women's Fashions

SKIRTS became even wider, supported by many more petticoats, with a small frilled pad or bustle tied on under the back gathers. Bonnets and hats were large.

The tightly fitting bodice was longer for all types of gowns, and it was usually back fastening throughout the thirties and forties. The V-shaped pleating or trimming on the bodice remained fashionable, also the wide neckline, which was often 'off the shoulder' for evening dress (Figs. 1, 5, 6). Frilled muslin tuckers were still worn (Figs. 3, 4), also frilled and embroidered muslin collars (Fig. 2) and the longer wide pelerine for daytime wear. The skirt stood out full from the bodice, being sewn in fairly wide, flat pleating; one of the petticoats underneath was usually piped, sometimes to just below knee-level, with the hem having a white embroidered flounce, making the dress itself spread out to a wide hemline. The use of ribbon and flowerlike decoration above the hem (Figs. 1, 5, 6) was discarded as the skirts widened during the later thirties.

The short puff sleeves for evening wear became really large (Figs. 5, 6), but the dinner dress often had long, fitting sleeves below the puff (Fig. 1). Daytime sleeves were long and full, particularly from 1830 to 1833, but from 1835 they usually fitted the arm nearly up to the elbow, with the sleeve full and puffed above, although it was often made fitting at the shoulder (Figs. 2, 3, 4). Poplin, printed cotton, silks, and fine cloths were used for day, with muslin still popular for evenings at first; silken gauze, organdie, and silk and satin also remained in fashion.

Cloaks, cashmere shawls, satin scarves, and muslin draperies continued in use.

The hair was similar in style, still dressed and curled fairly high on the head, although the side-ringlets were inclined to be longer by 1837.

Muslin caps, white-embroidered and frilled, continued for day wear, with large transparent hats for evening (Fig. 1); also the turban was still seen (Fig. 5). Wide-brimmed Leghorn hats (Fig. 4) or bonnets of silk had lavish decoration of bows, ribbons, and flowers, but by 1835 these became a little smaller (Figs. 2, 3).

Toes became more square, on the heelless pumps. For walking, heelless cloth ankle-boots, laced in front in the twenties, were by the thirties laced at the side.

Garters were a long, narrow strip of knitted wool tied above the knee, or the finest quality were of tiny brass-wire springs encased and sewn in silk; or from c. 1830 garters were of indiarubber woven 'elastic'.

Long kid gloves were usual with the short puff sleeve (Figs. 5, 6), and black silk mittens were fashionable day wear, but long white silk mittens became popular for evenings later; they were of net or openwork.

White was still fashionable, with often printed floral striped patterns for day, in fresh light colours; also mauve or lilac, soft pinks, blues and yellow, with white and yellow being popular for evening wear.

31

VICTORIA (1837–1901)

Men's Fashions

ALTHOUGH the top-hat remained as the most correct form of headwear, the bowler hat, cap, 'boater', and finally the Homburg hat appeared. More informal and looser-fitting coats and jackets as worn by sportsmen and the working classes considerably influenced the increasing popularity of more comfortable day clothes for men.

Frock-coat The frock-coat (Figs. 1, 11) was accepted as correct for everyday wear during the earlier part of this period, by all classes (Plate VII), and it continued to be used for more formal occasions until early in the twentieth century (p. 160, Fig. 2).

Cutaway coat During the early years, until the mid-forties, the cutaway riding-coat was still used for morning wear (p. 135 and p. 138, Fig. 1).

Morning-coat The morning-coat with the front sloped away at the sides (Fig. 10 and p. 154, Fig. 8) outlasted the frock-coat, being retained for formal occasions to the present day.

Evening coat By *c.* 1843 the blue evening coat with gilt buttons was being replaced by a black coat with dark buttons and dark pantaloons or trousers (Fig. 5); and before 1880 the evening coat was swallow-tailed, similar to that worn in the 1930's (p. 160, Fig. 11).

Jacket or lounge coat A short, loose-hanging jacket was worn as a form of lounge coat by 1860 (Fig. 14), and in the seventies it was cut even shorter and became increasingly popular (Fig. 9). It could be made with matching trousers, but more often coat, waistcoat, and trousers were each of a different material and colour. From the late forties to the seventies many morning-coats and lounge coats had the edges bound in braid, sometimes with the edges of the waistcoat bound as well.

Norfolk jacket and breeches From about the 1880's the 'Norfolk' jacket or sports coat (worn from the seventies), became much more fashionable; it had earlier been known as a 'shirt'. It was usually worn with loose, matching knee-breeches or knickerbockers (Fig. 6).

Waistcoat Brightly coloured waistcoats were seen until the sixties, with velvet or finely embroidered ones at first and with flowered or tartan ones in the forties and fifties, when they were single- or later double-breasted with wide lapels (Figs. 1, 5, 11). From 1860 waistcoats were often grey or made to match the coat; also by the sixties they were cut higher at the neck, so that little of the shirt-front was visible (Figs. 9, 14). Evening waistcoats were white (Fig. 5), and from 1880 were shorter to the waist; in the sixties and seventies they were often black, and these continued to be so when worn with the dinner jacket.

Neckwear In 1840 the collar was frequently turned down over the loosely knotted tie (Fig. 1), a fashion which became more general by 1870. Stiff, upright collars round the throat were worn in the nineties. Large bow-ties were fashionable in the earlier half of the reign (Fig. 2), but the smaller bow and the knotted tie were usual later. The frilled shirt-front was still worn with evening-dress at first (Fig. 5), but a plain, pleated shirt-

142

Victoria (1837~1901)

1 1842
2
3
4 1843
5 evening-dress
6 1899
7 1885
8
9 1892
10 1895
11 1849
12 1886
13 mid-19ᵗʰ cent.
14 1860~70

front was worn with the white bow-tie by 1870. A frilled shirt was revived in 1958.

Trousers The tight trousers (Figs. 1, 5) gradually became looser in cut. During the fifties and sixties plaid and check patterns were very popular (Fig. 14), but from the seventies plain grey or striped trousers were worn, and later dark striped trousers were correct for morning wear (Figs. 7, 10). Dark, tight, ankle-length trousers were worn for evening dress until about 1840, then black trousers were correct (Fig. 5).

It was still usual for trousers to be lighter in colour than the jacket (Plate VII), and they were not pressed or 'creased' until the '80's–'90's.

Shoes Lace-up shoes or short ankle-boots were worn (Fig. 13). Evening slippers were
Patent leather low cut during the earlier years (Fig. 5). Patent leather was used from the 1870's.
Overcoats Either single- or double-breasted overcoats were worn; in the forties they were tight-waisted with a full skirt; later loose-hanging coats were fashionable (Fig. 7); often the buttonholes were on an underflap, so that the buttons were hidden.

Hair Until about 1880 the hair was allowed to grow almost to a short bob (Figs. 1, 2, 5, 14), but by 1890 it was shorter and more closely shaven at the back and sides. The side-whiskers (Figs. 2, 14) became extremely long during the sixties, and were called
Dundreary Dundreary whiskers (Fig. 4). Beards were sometimes worn in the middle years (Fig. 6);
whiskers but moustaches remained in favour throughout this period.
Top-hat The top-hat was worn by all classes during the first half of Queen Victoria's reign, but was later used by middle and upper classes for formal wear (Figs. 7, 10).
Bowler In 1860 the black, stiff felt 'bowler' hat appeared (Fig. 14), and by 1876 it was as common as the top-hat. Brown or fawn bowlers were fashionable in 1890.
Cap Round cloth hats for sportsmen (Fig. 3) were later replaced by caps (Fig. 6).
Boater The straw 'boater' (Fig. 12) was seen in the summer, from 1885.
Homburg The light-coloured felt Homburg hat (Fig. 9) was occasionally worn instead of the 'bowler' or 'boater' during the last few years of the reign.
Smoking-cap Round caps, often embroidered, and made of velvet, etc. (Fig. 8), were worn
and jacket indoors by fashionable men in the middle years of the reign. Later only elderly men wore them. Short smoking-jackets were of velvet, cashmere, or patterned material.
Sticks, etc. Walking-sticks or umbrellas were carried. Spats were worn later (Figs. 6, 7).
Colours Until 1844 white trousers were fashionable with the blue frock-coat; then black coats and trousers were worn a great deal; also greys, browns, and navy; dark-green coats were sometimes seen at first with the check trousers. Later striped trousers in various shades of grey were correct, particularly with the jacket or the morning-coat (Fig. 10).

144

VICTORIA (1837–1901)

Women's Fashions: PART I (1837–60)

THE poke-bonnet and the crinoline were characteristic of the first part of Queen Victoria's reign, with richly patterned shawls displayed over widening skirts.

The lower-waisted bodice of the forties gave way to a slightly higher, rising waistline during the fifties and sixties. For evening wear the neckline was very low off the shoulders (Figs. 1, 2, 5), and during the fifties the bodice was often open down to the waist, showing the lace or muslin chemisette; this was also seen on the higher-necked day dresses (Figs. 7, 8). The very full flounced skirts of the fifties were usually separate from the bodice, which was often made in the form of a jacket (Figs. 3, 8). *Dresses*

Chemisette
Separate bodice

For day wear in the early forties sleeves were fitting to the wrist (Fig. 6); by the fifties they were worn shorter, often very wide, showing the puffed or frilled under-sleeves of white lace or embroidered muslin (Figs. 3, 7, 8). Puffed under-sleeves (Fig. 7) were very popular. A full bishop sleeve appeared on some dresses from 1855 to the sixties (Plate VII). *Sleeves*

At first the long full skirts were supported by a number of petticoats; then an underskirt of horsehair was worn under the petticoats, which were sometimes flounced, thus making the dresses stand out more stiffly from the waist. *Skirts*
Horsehair petticoat

By 1856 this was replaced by a petticoat with four or five quarter-inch steel hoops sewn above the hem, two to four inches apart, thus doing away with the need for so many bulky petticoats. Later, in 1857, there appeared a cage-like crinoline foundation, made of much finer steel hoops placed about three inches apart, being supported by wide tapes from the waist. It was left open a short way down the front. This fashion for extremely wide skirts was adopted by all classes. In the fifties the flounced skirt was the most popular for all types of dresses (Figs. 4, 5, 8), but plainer skirts returned in the sixties (Plate VII). Silks and poplins were for day wear, and printed muslins in the fifties; also wools, some as fine as muslins; white muslin or gauze for evenings in the fifties and sixties. Taffeta was for afternoon or dinner gowns; alpaca was sometimes used from 1841. Piped seams were very fashionable from the forties to the seventies, and fringe trimmings were popular in the fifties, also velvet and lace. Dresses were back fastening in the forties, usually hook and eye, with front fastenings in the fifties. *Crinoline*

Cage crinoline

Flounced skirt

Alpaca
Piped seams
Fastenings

Various types of mantles (Figs. 4, 6) were worn, with shot silk much used in the forties and fifties, also cloaks of taffeta, velvet, or cloth. Large cashmere shawls were extremely fashionable, also finely woven or printed Paisley and Norwich shawls and fringed ones of silk. *Mantles and cloaks*
Shawls

A tiny sleeved jacket, or 'bolero', was popular in 1853 and in the sixties (Plate VII) and nineties. *Bolero*

The hair was dressed smoothly back from the centre parting (Figs. 1, 3, 5, 8) or ringlets were very popular (Figs. 2, 6, 7). Hair

Victoria (1837-1901)
part 1 (1837-60)

1843
1

1841
2

1853
3

4
1853
-57

1857
5

1845
6

1850
7

1855
8

9

mid-19th cent.

Small muslin or lace caps were worn indoors and under the bonnet (Figs. 3, 6), particularly by married women.

Bonnets were smaller and almost flat across the top, being true 'poke-bonnets' (Figs. 4, 6, 7); in the fifties they became smaller still, especially in 1853; they showed more of the face and were set well on the back of the head (Fig. 3). Trimmings were of flowers, feathers, and lace, with ribbons of velvet or taffeta, on straw or silk bonnets, or velvet for winter. From c. 1857 younger women favoured round, fairly flat-brimmed straw hats for informal wear (seaside or gardening).

Black or white heelless pumps continued for formal wear, but tiny heels appeared on shoes and boots during the fifties (Fig. 9); boots were sometimes shaped for left and right feet, and, like the shoes, were made of satin, but cloth was used for walking, with toecaps and heels of black leather.

Mittens were worn in the thirties and forties, usually of black or white netted silk, long ones being for evening wear. In the fifties they were replaced by short kid gloves (Figs. 5, 7); these were generally white for evening.

Bags or reticules became less necessary with fully gathered skirts which were often made with concealed pockets in their folds or under their flounces from c. 1845 to 1855; but with lighter delicate fabrics in the later fifties and more smoothly fitting silks in the sixties, bags were again needed (Fig. 8), ones of brightly coloured 'Berlin woolwork' being popular. From c. 1835 to 1850 tiny purses to hold coins were usually entirely of bead-work, but steel beads were much used in the fifties and sixties. Stocking purses were a little longer.

Stockings were of white silk or cotton, the silk ones often having cotton tops; black stockings were usual with a black dress. Garters made of woven elastic (indiarubber) were commonly used from c. 1850.

Small folding carriage parasols were carried (Fig. 3), being very tiny in 1853. Also, to protect the complexion, an extra brim or 'ugly' was tied on to the front of the bonnet from 1848 to 1864.

White remained in favour for evening wear. In the forties soft shades of yellow, greenish gold, blues, and pinks were worn; but from the late forties stripes, plaids, and more brilliant shades of blues, greens, reds, and yellows came into fashion. Black, dark greens, purple, and browns with brighter-coloured trimmings were also seen in the fifties. Flowered brocaded silks were fashionable in the first few years; also flower sprays appeared on the striped silks and woollens in the forties to fifties with flower printed muslins particularly popular for the flounced dresses of the fifties, the flounces often being specially printed or even woven with deep borders of flowers to match the dress fabric. Plain shot silks became more fashionable in the later fifties to sixties, as the skirts spread over the crinoline frame and the flounced dress went out of fashion. Cloaks were of warmer tones such as dark red, brown or fawn, with white for evening wear.

Caps

Bonnets

Hats

Shoes and boots

Mittens and gloves

Bags and purses

Berlin woolwork

Bead purses

Stockings and garters

Parasols and the ugly

Colours

VICTORIA (1837–1901)
Women's Fashions : PART II (1860–85)

THE crinoline collapsed in the late sixties, and the bustle reappeared by the seventies. After fifty years the heeled shoe returned to favour; the sewing-machine, having been developed in America since 1845, came into general use during the sixties. Throughout the sixties and seventies the front-fastening bodice was shaped in to a tiny waist. The neckline was close round the throat at first but during the seventies a low, square neck opening or square trimming became usual (Figs. 5, 9); the high line returned by the eighties, with a standing collar (Figs. 6, 7, and Plate VII), which lasted to 1911. From 1874 the figure was stiffly corseted from shoulder to below hip-level; the day bodice, tightly fitting and boned, and extending over the hips, was at times made of a different material and was deeply pointed in front, a style called the cuirasse bodice. Evening gowns were low-necked with small puffed sleeves, but after 1875 they were often sleeveless. Skirts were generally longer than for day wear and trailed on the ground at the back, particularly during the years 1875–80.

From c. 1863 a separate top or blouse was worn with a belted skirt, with the blouse usually white or lighter in colour than the skirt.

Sleeves were long for day wear, usually edged with frills (Figs. 5, 8, 9), but during the sixties they were fairly close-fitting and plain, with a seam back and front. During the seventies they usually widened at the wrist (Figs. 4, 9, and Plate VII). From 1883 they were fitting (Fig. 7), and were frequently shorter to above the wrist.

At first the crinoline was dome-shaped (Fig. 1 and Plate VII); then front and sides were flatter, so that the skirt hung out to a wide hem (Fig. 8). The back was emphasized, often with long sash ends (Fig. 8), or with an overskirt looped up and back showing the underskirt, which could be of a different colour or was elaborately trimmed. The supporting cage crinoline of watch-spring steels lasted from 1857 to 1868; with the collapse of this foundation, winter 1867–68, when it was discarded, it left the unsupported skirts trailing on the ground. By 1869–70 the bustle returned to use; this time only the back half of the wire frame was necessary, or extra supporting steels were sometimes added to a small narrow crinoline frame, or 'crinolette', giving a protruding shape at the back only. Some were of an all-linen foundation, others, from 1870 to 1875, were of puffs and flounces on a horsehair fabric petticoat of varied lengths. The overskirt was often draped up and back to the bustle, giving an 'apron' effect in the seventies (Fig. 4), or this appearance was given by means of trimming (Fig. 5). Ruching and pleated frills were now lavishly used (Plate VII), and, owing to the invaluable use of the sewing-machine, dresses of 1875–90 were generally made of two different materials.

Between 1875 and 1880 the bustle became smaller and the fullness and puffs slipped half-way down the skirt (Fig. 9), with the front often arranged in tight folds from hip to knee. Tape-ties inside the back skirt controlled the drapery, both horizontally and often vertically when the low bustle consisted of a series of puffs (Plate VII).

148

Victoria (1837 – 1901)
part II (1860-85)

widow's cap and veil

1
1860

2
1860
-70

3
1876

4
1870-
75

1870

5

6

1885
7

1868
8

9
1875-
80

Trained
dresses
Tournure, or
*dress-
improver*
Tailor-mades

All skirts trailed on the ground from the mid-seventies, but for day wear by the eighties they were shorter, being ground-length all round (Plate VII).

By 1881 the bustle again rose upward, and by 1885 it stood more sharply out at the back than before (Fig. 7), being supported on a narrower bustle or 'tournure', or 'dress-improver'. The skirt without trimming hung in rich folds at the back.

From 1877 costumes for morning or country wear were being 'tailor-made'. Dresses at first were of silks and taffeta, with striped cottons and silks in the seventies and eighties. Woollen cloths, alpaca, and velvet were worn, with velvet for trimmings. Muslin and organdie were for evening wear, also silk, satin and velvet, and net over silk.

Shawls
*Reversible
shawls*
Coats and
dolman jacket
Hair

At first lace shawls were most fashionable over the plain spreading skirts of the sixties, with woven or printed reversible shawls in the late sixties. Also then, various half- or threequarter-length coats were popular (Fig. 1). In the eighties a mantle or dolman jacket, with short sleeve from elbow to wrist only, had the back shaped to fall over the bustle; this reached from hip to mid-thigh and was used for day or evening.

Hair hung full at the back up to the seventies, being coiled above or on the nape of the neck (Fig. 1), or ringlets were still seen at first (Fig. 8). A coarse net covering the mass of hair at the back was used a great deal (Figs. 1, 2); sometimes false hair was added

to this 'chignon', being attached by means of a comb. The coils and plaits looped up on the back of the head were very large in the seventies (Figs. 4, 5, 9), but during the eighties hair was dressed close to the head, arranged in a small neat coil on top (Fig. 7).

In the early sixties the bonnet became very small, with the sides cut away, showing the lace and hair, but the top projected forward over the forehead in a 'spoon' shape; by the seventies the bonnet was only discernible from the hat in that it had ribbons tied

under the chin (Figs. 4, 9). These and many tiny hats were usually trimmed with flowers, feathers, and ribbons (Fig. 8). Hats were set well forward on the head; a small plain straw, feather-trimmed (Fig. 1), and the plain round 'pork-pie' (Fig. 2) were popular in the sixties, with a straw or felt Tyrolean shape in the seventies (Fig. 3). In the eighties both hats and bonnets were set flat on top of the head, being usually small in size.

White silk or cotton stockings were correct for formal wear until the seventies, but with the increasing use of coloured ones in the sixties, some even being striped, the use of coloured ones matching the dress became acceptable for evening wear from the seventies; open-work or embroidered ones were fashionable in the seventies and eighties.

Heeled shoes were shaped for left and right feet, and, like the stockings, were often coloured from the sixties, matching the dress. The curved 'Louis' heel appeared from the seventies on, when toes became more pointed; bronze kid became very fashionable.

The plainer parasols of the sixties had short, thick handles, but these increased in length in the seventies (Fig. 9), with elaboration of both handle and parasol itself.

Dark serge bathing-dresses, with trousers, were calf-length and were trimmed with pleats, braid, and buttons. Corsets were worn; hats were of ribbon and straw.

Generally, at first, and for evenings, colours were delicate, white, blue, grey, lilac, pink, and pale brown; trimmings were often dark, such as black on soft pink and white, or bright blue on pale green-grey. Plain or shot silks, or small neat patterns or stripes in the sixties, with stripes in stronger contrasting colours in the seventies and eighties, when dresses of two colours and two textiles were usual. Greens, mauve, golden fawn, blue, purple, brown, red, and black, with darker colours in 1870–71. In the eighties, colours were harsh and strong.

VICTORIA (1837–1901)

Women's Fashions: PART III (1885–1901)

THE bustle went out of fashion; the long skirt, heavy with back drapery, was hooked to a separate boned bodice, and huge 'leg-of-mutton' sleeves appeared in the nineties.

The bodice was well tailored, and every seam was boned in an attempt to keep the waist as small as possible; it was usually made pointed in front (Figs. 1, 2, 4) and finished well below the normal waistline; evening dresses usually fastened at the back, and day dresses in front, but the skirt placket was invariably concealed in the back folds of the skirt; hooks and eyes were used; snap fasteners were invented in 1890.

For day wear the standing collar was high (Figs. 2, 3, 6), but fairly low necks, either square or rounded, were usual for evening dresses (Fig. 4), when a choker necklace was worn round the throat. Frills of lace were used a great deal, accentuating the width of the shoulders on both high- and low-necked dresses (Fig. 4). The shoulders of the long, tight sleeves were emphasized in the late eighties (p. 149, Fig. 7), with the upper part at the shoulder raised in 1892 (Fig. 7); this puff or fullness (Figs. 2, 3) developed after 1893 into the huge gigot or 'leg-of-mutton' sleeve of 1895 and 1896 (Fig. 6). It was very fully gathered on the shoulder, but fitting on the forearm to wrist; the fullness collapsed in 1897, and by 1898 sleeves were more normally shaped at the shoulder (p. 157, Figs. 1, 9). Large puff sleeves, with or without lace frills, were usual on evening dress.

From 1887 the bustle began to shrink, and it disappeared entirely by 1888–89 (Fig. 2). The front of the skirt was still flounced (Fig. 1) or draped (Fig. 2) until 1890; and day dresses became much more trim and a little shorter, especially for holiday wear and sport, etc. (Fig. 5), but long, trailing skirts returned by the end of the reign (Figs. 4, 6). Evening gowns remained very long, and often had two or three flounces at the hem; note the extra fan-shaped piece accentuating the back of Fig. 4. Woollen cloths were now used much more for day dresses, also silk and cloth. Silks and satin were used for afternoon and evening wear. Evening gowns often had a gauze overskirt and satin bodice; trimmings (such as sleeves and hem) of velvet or lace and chiffon were fashionable in the nineties, and skirts were silk-lined.

Towards the end of the reign short open jackets reaching to the hips were worn with a separate skirt and a blouse (Fig. 5) which was pouched over the skirt at the waist; the front could be plain or frilled; lace frills were very fashionable.

Well-tailored, full- or threequarter-length coats were popular (Fig. 7); also various flared capes, short, covering the shoulders, or longer to hip-level, were seen a great deal in the nineties, when the bolero also appeared again.

The hair was dressed close to the head, but towards the end of the reign it was fuller in the front, often with curls fluffed and frizzed over the forehead, and with the

Side notes:
Dresses
Bodice and fastenings

Snap-fasteners
Standing collar

Sleeves

Raised sleeve
Leg-of-mutton sleeve

Skirt

Jacket
Blouse

Coats
Capes and boleros

Hair

Victoria (1837-1901)
part III (1885-1901)

1887
1

1889
2

1889-93
3

4

5

6
1892
1896

7

9 1885
first style of handbag
produced commercially

1898
8

1893
evening dress

coil on top of the head (Figs. 3, 4). Small pads were used under the front hair to give it extra height and width.

Very small bonnets were still worn (Fig. 1), also flat hats (Fig. 2), with trimmings of ribbons, flowers, and feathers, and from 1890 small jet ornaments were added. Almost brimless hats were perched forward on the head (Fig. 5), sometimes with veils that were drawn tightly over the face and fastened up to the hat at the back. *Hats*

From about 1896 hats were very flat and set on top of the head, being held in position with hatpins (Fig. 6); straw boaters (similar to Fig. 8) were also worn for cycling, walking, etc. *Hatpins* *Boaters*

For cycling in 1894–96, short, well-tailored coats reaching to above the knee were worn with full knickerbockers (similar to male breeches), which were fastened below the knee; button-up leggings completed the outfit; but skirts were more usual among the better-class women, who took up cycling when it was new and a novelty; they considered skirts were more ladylike. They gave up this form of exercise when the 'lower orders' took to cycling. *Knicker-bockers*

Leather handbags were first produced commercially in 1885 (Fig. 9); soon a great variety of elegant styles were being manufactured, some containing sections holding needles, scissors, and thread, and manicure outfits, in addition to the usual purse and mirror (Figs. 2, 7). *Handbags*

Shoes and boots had pointed toes and medium-sized curved 'Louis' heels. Fashionable shoes had two or more bars over the instep, and at first the toe was bead-embroidered. Black lace-up shoes and lace-up and button-up boots to above the ankle (Fig. 8) were usual for walking or street wear. Soft bronze kid was popular for shoes, also black or fawn with white for summer dresses and for evenings, when shoes were often of coloured satin, matching the dress. *Shoes and boots*

In the eighties and nineties open-work stockings were much used for evening wear, also embroidered ones in the eighties, when ribbed stockings were popular for day wear. By the nineties black ones were worn for day or evening, only for full dress white ones were correct. *Stockings*

Small muffs were used a great deal in cold weather. *Muffs*

Brooches were very fashionable. With evening dress, rows of pearls encircling the throat were very popular. *Jewellery*

Stripes and plaids were still worn during the day in the eighties, also two materials in one dress (Fig. 2); then harsh blues, greens, and deep reds were worn, also very soft pale greys and fawns. Colours were more delicate for the evenings, such as white, pinks, or white with deep-red sleeves and hem or soft green trimmed with mauve. *Colours*

Edward VII
(1901-10)

1906
1

1901
2

bathing-
dress

3

4

1907
5

1905
6

7
1906

8
1910

9

10
1910

32

EDWARD VII (1901–10)

Men's Fashions

THE top-hat and morning-coat were worn by the well-dressed man for business, etc., but the bowler hat and short jacket were otherwise most usual.

The frock-coat was still worn by the older men (see p. 160, Fig. 2) instead **Coats** of the more fashionable morning-coat (Fig. 8). The short jacket which was worn by all classes (Fig. 9) retained the short slit at the back, though the pleats had long since disappeared. The lighter-coloured jacket or lounge coat of flannel or tweed could either be plain or belted (Figs. 1, 10), and the Norfolk or sports coat was pleated and belted as before (Fig. 7). Evening coats similar to Fig. 11, p. 160, remained with little alteration for almost fifty years.

Waistcoats were made to match the coat (Figs. 8, 9), but in the summer light ones **Waistcoat** were common with the lounge coat. Evening waistcoats were white or black.

The plain, stiff, upright collar (Fig. 4) was still occasionally seen at first, and also **Neckwear** the wing collar (Fig. 8), which was worn with the morning-coat and evening dress. The stiff turned-down collar with bow or tie was most usual (Figs. 1, 3, 5, 7, 10). White or black bow-ties were worn with evening coats, but white was later correct.

Trousers were fairly narrow and were usually short to the ankle with 'turn-ups'. **Trousers** Dark striped ones were worn with the morning-coat and short black jacket (Figs. 8, 9). Otherwise they were grey (Fig. 10) or made to match the lounge coat (Fig. 1). Knee-breeches were worn by sportsmen (Fig. 7).

Both shoes and short boots were worn, and spats were considered correct with the **Shoes** morning-coat (Fig. 8) until the end of the reign.

Overcoats were little changed, being either single- or double-breasted; astrakhan **Overcoats** collars were sometimes worn by the wealthier men in the winter (Fig. 5).

Waterproof coats were also worn; they usually had a Raglan sleeve (similar to *Waterproof* Fig. 7, p. 160), and the buttonholes were on an under-flap down the front of the coat, *coat* so that the buttons were hidden. The Inverness cape of Victorian times was sometimes seen in 1905 (Fig. 6). After that it was no longer fashionable.

The hair was short and fairly well trimmed at the back and sides. Moustaches were **Hair** quite fashionable; short beards were sometimes seen on elderly men (Fig. 6).

Top-hats were worn by professional and well-dressed businessmen (Figs. 6, 8), **Hats** and also for formal morning wear. Bowler hats were very common (Figs. 3, 5, 9), even tram-drivers wearing them in 1902. From 1904 the boater was extremely popular for the summer, in town or country (Fig. 10). Both the Homburg (Fig. 4) and the cap (Figs. 1, 7) were worn much more.

Men's bathing-costumes reached to the knees; striped ones were very common. **Bathing-**
costume
Black coats with striped trousers were worn by businessmen, lounge coats, etc., **Colours** were of greys or darker shades of brown or navy.

155

EDWARD VII (1901–10)

Women's Fashions

E XTREMELY large, wide hats and trailing skirts dominated the early years of the twentieth century. Fashions were designed for the mature woman with the Edwardian S-bend silhouette. But the straighter sheath-line of 1909, followed by the 'hobble' skirt of 1910, put an end to the frothy, beribboned petticoats previously so popular.

Dresses   Until 1908 the curve of the figure was accentuated by the straight-fronted corset and the fullness of the bodice, which was pouched over the belt in front (Figs. 4, 10, and Plate VIII). The neckline with the standing collar was high round the throat, being held up by the tiny bone or wire supports, which were also used on the tucked net or lace

Guimpe   guimpe (Figs. 4, 8, 9). Evening dresses were low-necked (Figs. 6, 10). Waists were small, and the figure was corseted to well down over the hips. Wide collars, capes or frills or

Snap   pleated trimmings on the bodice were V-shaped (Figs. 4, 6, 8, 10); these were often

fasteners   identical back and front, particularly in 1907–12. Snap fasteners were increasingly used.

Sleeves   From 1903–4 the fairly fitting sleeve was often pouched just below the elbow and gathered into a fitting band at the wrist (Fig. 4); or a full, wide, flounced trimming hung from an elbow-length sleeve in 1907–8, which was popular at that time. Under-sleeves of tucked net or lace, matching the guimpe, were frequently worn with this length sleeve (Figs. 8, 9). Full, puffed sleeves were also fashionable about 1907 (Fig. 6).

Blouse   Blouses were worn a great deal (Figs. 1, 7), silk, lace, or crocheted ones being most fashionable in 1907 with smart tailored outfits (Fig. 9).

.Tea-gown   No fashionable woman was without a tea-gown, which by 1908 had reached the ultimate in a trailing luxury of lace and frills. When first worn in c. 1877, as a loose dress, without corsets, by married women only, it was a form of elegant dressing-gown. By the eighties, young women were wearing it, and soon it became as fashionable as an afternoon or evening dress.

Skirt   At first skirts were long, trailing on the ground at the back (Figs. 4, 9, and Plate VIII), usually with some form of decoration on the wide, spreading hemline, often with lace, frills, ribbons, and tucks almost up to knee-level on some of the more elaborate dresses. The skirt was gored, with fullness flaring out from centre back, even tailored costumes sweeping the floor; skirts for sport remained a fraction shorter (Figs. 1, 7).

Sheath gown   In 1909 a slender form-fitting dress from Paris appeared; high-waisted and high-necked, with long, fitting sleeves, it flowed from a graceful, sheath-like gown to a narrow yet trailing hemline. Voluminous petticoats and stiff corsets could not be worn with this dress, and many older women found it did not suit their figures.

Hobble skirt   But skirts had already begun to shorten in 1908 (Fig. 10), and by 1910 the 'hobble' skirt appeared (Fig. 11), being narrower and more restrictive than anything worn before. Many skirts had a small slit at front or side, to make walking easier. But it quickly

Edward VII (1901-10)

1901
1

2
bathing-dress

3

4 1904

1907
5

6
1905
-07

1906
cyclist
7

8

9
1902
-07

10

1908
evening dress

11
1910

became very fashionable, although the flared skirt remained for sportswear (Fig. 7).

Tailored
costumes

Tailored walking costumes followed the fashionable trend, with waisted, hip-length coats and fitting sleeve, although elbow-length puffed sleeves were seen *c.* 1907.

Velveteen

Day or afternoon dresses were of velvet, velveteen, cashmere, delaine, and wool crêpes, also muslin, lace, or net over silk for afternoon wear. Woollen cloths and serge were used for skirts or costumes (Figs. 1, 7, 9). Silks were worn more from 1908, also crêpe-de-chine. For evening wear, silks, satin, and light materials, tulle, chiffon, or lace over satin were used. Embroidery and trimmings, tucks, lace, frills, and ribbons were lavishly used on the trailing dresses.

*Crêpe-de-
chine*

Coats

Coats were long or three-quarter length (Figs. 3 and Plate VIII), usually well tailored, although a straight-hanging thigh-length coat was sometimes worn for walking *c.* 1901, and an ample, nearly full-length raglan-sleeved coat was fashionable for motoring in 1907. Fitting and belted coats were seen towards 1910. Fur coats were worn by the wealthier women (Fig. 5), whose cloth coats were often embroidered (Plate VIII).

Motoring coat
Fur coats

Bolero

The short bolero jacket was fashionable again about 1902, with the popular three-quarter or elbow-length sleeve (Fig. 9); it had previously appeared in the 1890's and from 1853 to the 1860's.

Hair

The hair was piled on top of the head, with the front puffed and padded out (Fig. 6); both pads and false hair were used, particularly towards 1908, forming quite a firm foundation for the huge hats of this period.

Hats

At first the elaborately trimmed hats were of a fairly large size, with the trimming often making them appear taller than their width (Figs. 5, 8), and they were usually balanced on top of the head, being secured with large hatpins. From *c.* 1903 hats increased in width, reaching immense proportions by 1910 (Figs. 3, 4, 9, 11). Toques of velvet or feathers were also worn (Fig. 5), and veils were fashionable with these and other up-turned shapes (Fig. 8); veils were used to secure the very large hats when motoring or at seaside resorts (Fig. 3). Sportswomen wore boaters or small flat hats (Figs. 1, 7).

Toque

Boaters
Shoes

Strap shoes with moderate curved heels were fashionable (Figs. 7, 11).

Gloves

Long, elbow-length gloves were worn with the shorter sleeves (Fig. 11), or extra half-sleeves of lace or net, reaching from elbow to wrist, could be put on for outdoor wear. Then only short gloves were necessary. For evening dress long white gloves reached to the elbow.

Parasols

Parasols, like the large summer hats, were still used to protect the Englishwoman's complexion from the sun. They were an elegant and important accessory, being frilled or lace-covered, and were frequently made to match the dress (Fig. 9 and Plate VIII).

Feather boas

Feather boas were most popular (Fig. 8), also muffs (Plate VIII); delicate lace scarves were worn in the summer.

Bathing-
costumes

Bathing-dresses were shorter and not so restricted or elaborately trimmed (Fig. 2). They were made with or without skirts. The hat was waterproof and more simple.

Colours

Blacks and greys were usual for the first year or two, then red was much worn, also navy and cream and many shades of delicate fawns, pinks, blues, and soft greens, trimmed with pale contrasting colours, such as biscuit with light green. White was worn for evenings or afternoon summer dresses, also other pastel colours trimmed with sequins, ribbons, or flowers. Both white and black lace were popular, also embroidered net—for example, black net trimmed with lace and ribbon could be worn over a bright yellow silk taffeta under-dress.

158

33

GEORGE V (1910–36)

Men's Fashions

THE lounge suit and trilby hat became increasingly popular; the black Homburg, commonly known as the 'Anthony Eden' hat, tended to replace the bowler. Breeches developed into 'plus-fours'.

Business and professional men wore the morning-coat until 1914 (see p. 154, Fig. 8); after that it was used for formal occasions. The frock-coat (Fig. 2) was sometimes worn by elderly men. The black jacket and pin-striped trousers continued to be correct for businessmen, though later dark lounge suits were often worn instead. In the early twenties the jacket was either single- or double-breasted (Figs. 9, 10); the former was generally used for summer wear. Finely striped cloth was usual for lounge suits; also plain cloth and navy serge. Tweed sports coats were worn a great deal (Fig. 9), and brightly coloured 'blazers' (Fig. 3).

The evening coat was little changed (Fig. 11), but after the First World War it was used more for dances, otherwise the single-breasted dinner-jacket was worn.

The waistcoat was made to match the coat. For evening wear it was white with the tailed coat (Fig. 11), but black with the dinner-jacket.

Knitted pullovers replaced waistcoats with the sports jacket (Fig. 8).

The stiff wing collar was correct with evening dress (Fig. 11), though some older men still wore it during the day (Fig. 2). The plain stiff collar was usual, but the soft collar matching the shirt became very popular during the thirties (Figs. 8, 9). The tie was more fashionable than the bow-tie, except for evening wear, when a white bow-tie was correct with the tailed coat and a black one with the dinner-jacket. Open-neck shirts were usual for holiday wear, tennis, cricket, etc. (Fig. 3).

Trousers remained rather narrow until the mid-twenties, when for a short while young men favoured very wide grey flannels, called 'Oxford bags' (Fig. 9). For nearly twenty years following this fashion trousers were of a more moderate width and length (Figs. 7, 10). Grey flannels or matching trousers were worn with the tweed sports coat, and white flannels were used for tennis or cricket (Fig. 3); but by 1936 white shorts were often used for tennis. Plus-fours came in during the early twenties (Fig. 8); they were of tweed to match the coat and were chiefly worn for golf, but even for that purpose grey flannels later became more popular.

Shoes replaced the short boots after the First World War.

Single- or double-breasted overcoats were fashionable (Figs. 6, 7, 10).

Throughout this period lightweight fawn-coloured mackintoshes were used; they were plain or belted (Fig. 5). Women often wore belted mackintoshes.

The hair was very well trimmed at the back and sides; the face was clean-shaven, but many men favoured small moustaches.

The silk hat continued to be worn with the morning (or frock) coat until about

Coats

Lounge suit

Dinner-jacket
Waistcoat

Pullovers
Neckwear

Trousers
Oxford bags

Shorts
Plus-fours

Shoes
Overcoats
Mackintosh

Hair

Hats

159

George V (1910–36)

1914 1   2 1914   3   4   1935   5   6   1936   7

early 1920's 8

9 1924 -26

10

11

evening-dress

1914 (Fig. 2). After that it was seen on formal occasions or with evening dress only (Fig. 11). The dull-surfaced, collapsible opera hat was also used with evening dress. In the thirties the bowler (Fig. 5) was often replaced by the Homburg (Fig. 6). The trilby (Fig. 10) and the Homburg were very common. A round-shaped felt, called the 'pork-pie' hat (Fig. 7), was seen at the end of the reign, when both this and the trilby were of grey, green, or brown. The boater was worn in the summer until 1914, and it had a brief revival in 1930 (Fig. 1). The cap, in plain or check cloth, was worn by the sporting man (Fig. 8), also by workmen.

Trilby
'Pork-pie'
hat

After the First World War men's bathing-costumes gradually became shorter to the top of the thigh; they were sleeveless with round-shaped necks. But by about 1935 they were generally replaced by trunks (Fig. 4).

Bathing-costume

Black, navy, and dark shades of browns and greys were worn throughout this period. Tweeds were in lighter colours, in various shades of browns, red-browns, fawns, blue-greens, and greys. Then, later, brighter and richer tones were fashionable. Pullovers were often brightly coloured, but in the thirties were of rich soft shades of deep reds, greens, blues, and browns, also grey. Shirts, either plain or finely striped, were of pale blue, grey, fawn, or white; but at the end of this period greens and fresher colours were more popular.

Colours

GEORGE V (1910–36)

Women's Fashions: PART I (1910–28)

DRASTIC changes took place in women's dress. The hem, waist, and neckline were all altered; large hats gave way to small ones; hair was cut short, and it became fashionable for women to wear skirts only to knee-level.

Dresses

A high-waisted 'Empire' line was seen in 1910–14, when there was also a normal waist-level which lasted until the early twenties (Figs. 1, 2, 3, 11), though coat-belts, as in Fig. 2, were often worn round the hips from 1915, children having had a low-waisted style since the late 1890's (p. 152, Fig. 8). By 1923 all dresses were practically waistless, hanging straight down with the belt low on the hips (Fig. 10); the front and back were often identical, and there were no fastenings on many of them. Within two years the high collar (Fig. 1), popular for so long, was replaced by a moderate V shape (Fig. 3 and Plate VIII) and the straighter boat-shaped neck (Figs. 2, 10, 11), which was also worn on evening dresses, although it later became more rounded (Fig. 12). By 1922 blouses and the new knitted woollen cardigan (Fig. 4) reached hip-level.

Low waist

Blouse and cardigan

Sleeves

Long or elbow-length sleeves were usual; the wider type (Figs. 10, 13) came into fashion soon after 1920. Evening dresses were sleeveless in the twenties (Fig. 12).

Skirt

The 'hobble' skirt remained in vogue until 1915 (Figs. 1, 3), but the flared skirt continued to be worn by the more energetic women (Fig. 4); and during the war years 1914–18 this wide, 'easy-to-wear' style became usual, although it was worn a little shorter above the ankle (Plate VIII). Up to 1914 short overskirts or tunics of thin material or lace were fashionable for day or evenings (Fig. 1); they were of knee-length usually, and fuller than the slim skirt underneath, and were often cut or draped up in front. During the war years the long, narrow skirt was discarded, and dresses by the early twenties reached to just below the calf (Fig. 11).

Jumper frock

Coat-frock

At this time the practical jumper frock or 'pinafore' dress appeared (Plate VIII), also the coat-frock, and the shorter evening dresses were often deeply scalloped at the hem.

From 1923 to 1925 straight-hanging and slightly longer dresses were worn (Fig. 10), and the skirt was at times draped round the hips to a large decorative buckle or beaded panel at the front or side, and evening frocks often had longer, floating side-panels. There was an Egyptian influence in both decoration and colour from 1923.

Egyptian influence

Short skirts

By 1926 skirts for all occasions were short to just below the knee; dance frocks had rounded or pointed scalloped hems or inserted flared pieces, giving the popular 'handkerchief' skirt (Fig. 12) seen during the next four or five years, although by 1930, with hemlines lengthening again, the points were long to the ankles, with the slip underneath knee-length and later calf-length. Knee-length, pleated skirts were fashionable for day wear *c.* 1927, also a slim, straight, narrow skirt (Fig. 13).

Handkerchief skirt

Pleated skirt

Materials

White muslin was still used for cool summer dresses until 1914; silks, velveteen, and fine woollen cloths were also as before. Serge was used a great deal from 1914 to 1918

162

George V (1910-36)   part I (1910-28)

1912
1

1915
2

1914
3

1914
4

5
'21

1925
6

7
'24

8
'28

1927
9

10
1925

11
1922

12
1927
-29

13
1927
-29

evening dress

and for several years afterwards. In the twenties stockinette or knitted costumes and dresses of silk and wool were worn, also marocain, velveteen, printed cottons, shantung, crêpe-de-chine, and lace for afternoon or evening wear. Georgette, satin, and taffeta were for evening dresses, but beaded dresses were the height of fashion in 1924–28, either on part only (Fig. 12) or completely covering the whole fabric.

Three-quarter-length coats were worn (Figs. 3, 13), and at first were well tailored to the waist, sometimes with a curved cutaway front, when worn with the hobble skirt. By 1916 many straight, waistless coats were seen, from half-length casual (Fig. 2) or costume coats to those of full length (Figs. 5, 10). The style of collar on Figs. 8, 13 was typical of the later twenties.

Until 1913 the hair was dressed fairly full as before, but it was then arranged closer to the head and curled or waved forward round the face (Fig. 3 and Plate VIII) and coiled lower at the back of the head. Short bobbed hair was sometimes seen during the First World War, but it did not become general until the twenties. By 1924 the back was 'shingled' (Fig. 12), with front and sides closely waved; the closer-cut 'Eton crop' appeared in 1926, but this extreme mode was less popular than the shingle.

As previously, the shape of the hat was dictated by the hair style. From 1910 to 1912 hats remained huge (Fig. 1), then tall, feather-trimmed, close-fitting ones were fashionable (Figs. 3, 5), followed by a smaller crowned shape with a tiny curved brim (Fig. 2), or others with a very wide, flat, straight brim. During 1914–17 hats were often tilted over one eye as in the thirties; feather trimmings were used until early in the twenties. By 1922 the crown was deepening with a dipping brim at the sides (Fig. 11), and by 1924 very close-fitting hats became extremely popular (Fig. 7). These 'cloche' hats, worn over the short-cut hair, could be with or without brims (Figs. 8, 10, 13), and were pulled right down over the eyebrows.

At first black stockings were worn as before, but by 1921–22 flesh-pinks were being worn; some, which had appeared ten years earlier, had been considered rather daring. But in the twenties, with shorter skirts and the use of rayon, stockings became a brighter pink and more shiny in appearance, as the skirts rose upward.

Strap shoes were usual at first (Fig. 3), also high-heeled shoes with a large tongue and buckle (Figs. 10, 11). Plain court shoes became increasingly popular (Fig. 13), replacing the single-strap shoe (Fig. 12). Ankle-length boots were worn until c. 1918.

Medium-sized handbags were carried until the mid-twenties (Fig. 10), when a flat handle-less, pochette style was introduced (Fig. 13); these were sometimes 'zip'-fastened along the top from 1924, when this new-style metal-slide fastener was being manu-factured.

From 1925 to 1927 the design and colour of bathing-dresses changed: from dark knee-length ones they became gay, sleeveless, and short (Figs. 6, 9).

Summer afternoon dresses and blouses were white in 1910–14, with lace and em-broidery. Fresh light colours and pastel shades of pre-war years gave way to darker and more sombre shades, brown, fawn, blue, and navy, until after 1918. Then came soft beige and peach colours with rich orange-reds, tan and golden yellows in the twenties. Following the discovery of Tutankhamen's tomb, late 1922, colours became brilliant, particularly for evening wear, with bead decoration. Black was fashionable in the mid-twenties, for lace afternoon or evening wear. Greys, brown, navy, soft reds, blues, and greens were for day wear.

GEORGE V (1910–36)

Women's Fashions: PART II (1928–36)

SKIRTS were of a more moderate length by 1930, with a normal waistline. Backless bathing-dresses, beach pyjamas, and shorts appeared.

The low waist remained in fashion until the end of 1929 (Fig. 10). Then all dresses had normal waistlines. The neck was V-shaped or rounded (Figs. 3, 6, 10), but towards the end of the reign slightly higher-necked day dresses were more fashionable (Figs. 7, 9). After 1930 evening gowns were cut much lower at the back, and by 1935 they were low to the waist (Fig. 11). In 1928 brightly coloured scarves were worn, knotted at the front; after 1935 scarves (a little less gaudy) tied at the back or looped in the front were often seen under the coat (Fig. 8). *Dresses*

The long sleeves were more fitting until 1935, when they were often made fuller, as in Figs. 4, 12. Sleeveless summer dresses were frequently worn until 1930 (Fig. 2), when puffed sleeves became popular (Figs. 7, 9). Plain short ones, as in Fig. 1, were worn with more tailored dresses. Evening gowns were sleeveless (Fig. 11). *Sleeves*

All dresses were shorter to above the knee in 1928 (Fig. 10), except for elderly women. Evening dresses in that year were often longer at the back to below the knee. By 1929 a 'flutter' hemline reached nearly to the ankle; then in 1930 long skirts returned for formal occasions (Fig. 3). Day dresses too became longer (Fig. 6), until by 1935–36 they were half-way between the calf and the ankle, as in Figs. 4, 9, 12. *Skirt* / *Dropped* and *flutter hemlines*

A number of new materials were worn, and in 1934 uncrushable velvets, linens, etc., were introduced; artificial silks were much used from 1930. The richer and more delicate fabrics and gold and silver tissues were used for evening dresses. *Uncrushable materials*

Long coats (Figs. 8, 10, 12) and short, tailored costume coats (Fig. 6) were worn. From about 1932 three-quarter-length coats, hanging loose and full from shoulder to hem, called 'swagger coats', were also in vogue (Fig. 4). Tweed cloths were often used. Costumes of uncrushable linen were often worn in the summer. *Coats* / *Swagger coats*

Shingled hair was fashionable until the thirties (Figs. 1, 2), but in 1929 it was often longer with a row of curls round the nape of the neck. From then until 1936 it was fairly short and beautifully waved and curled (Figs. 7, 8, 9, 11). *Hair*

The 'cloche' hat was made even closer-fitting in 1928 (Fig. 10); then hats with brims were favoured again, and in the summer they were often quite large with a drooping brim (Fig. 3); from 1932 the crown was made smaller and the brim flatter and curved (Fig. 7). In 1931 'bowler' hats with a small, curved brim were seen. Then variously shaped hats, berets, and shaped cloth hats were worn placed well over one eye (Figs. 4, 6, 12). Taller crowned hats were fashionable from 1934 (Fig. 8), and halo hats appeared (Fig. 9). A small, brimless cap, called the 'Juliet' hat, was also very common, similar to Fig. 6e, p. 172. *Hats* / *Bowler* / *Beret* / *Halo-hats* / *Juliet hat*

Silk and artificial-silk stockings of shades of suntan and fawns were worn. *Stockings*

165

George V (1910-36)
part II
(1928-36)

1930 1
'29 2
3 1930
4 1936
1933 5
1931 6
7
8 1934
1935 9
garden-party dress
10 1928
11 1935
12 1936
evening dress

High-heeled court shoes were very popular (Figs. 4, 6, 10, 12). Dainty lace-up shoes and occasionally strap shoes were also worn. Sandal shapes were seen later for summer and evening wear (Figs. 9, 11). Coloured leathers and suèdes were used. Low-heeled strap or lace-up shoes were for walking in town or country (Fig. 1).

Short, round-necked, sleeveless bathing-dresses (now plain-coloured) were replaced, in 1933, by the backless type (Fig. 5) in brighter and soft pastel shades.

Black or khaki shorts (Fig. 1) were introduced from America in 1930; by 1932–33 they were popular with hikers and girl-cyclists. White shorts for tennis were also often favoured.

In 1931 brightly coloured beach pyjamas became popular. The trousers were wide, and the upper part was backless. Pyjamas for home wear were also in vogue. The top was loosely cut with wide sleeves; the trouser leg was very full, giving almost the appearance of a skirt.

Fastenings for dress or skirt were at the side-waist, of the snap-fastener type, which were sewn on individually. These were small and neat, obtainable in various sizes, and incorporated a double S spring, insuring good closure, being much improved since the earlier, larger ones made during the First World War. Hooks and eyes were still used, but the snap fasteners became more popular for dress or petticoat. Zip fasteners were more for handbags and items such as pockets, boots, or bags of thick material or leather, the zips at that time being of metal and rather heavy.

In 1929 geometric designs and brilliant colours were replaced by plainer colours; and from early in the thirties innumerable rich pastel shades were fashionable. Summer dresses were plain or of small-flowered patterns, etc., of many delicate shades of yellows (peach, sun-tan, etc.), blues, turquoise, greens, yellow-greens, pinks, and beige or grey. Black was much worn in the winter, also navy and white, tan colour, and darker shades of browns, reds, blues, greens, pale grey, and fawn.

34

GEORGE VI (1936–52)—ELIZABETH II (1952–)

Men's Fashions : PART I (1936–56)

Teddy boys

Coats

Utility

Drape

Proofed gaberdine

Zip fastener

Waistcoat

Sweaters

Shirt

Nylon

Trousers

THE reign of Edward VIII in 1936 has been included in that of George VI.
During this period there were noticeable changes in the cut of men's clothes.
After the Second World War there was a return to a certain Edwardian formality as well as an increased informality for leisure wear. An extreme form of Edwardianism was affected by youths, chiefly in the larger cities: they became known as 'teddy boys' (Fig. 9).

The general cut of the lounge coat and sports jacket remained little altered until the late forties, being single- or double-breasted, with a fairly built-up shoulder and wide lapel. A 'Utility' suit was introduced in 1942; the jacket was shorter (Fig. 2), had no waist pleats or breast pocket or buttons on the cuff, and no buckles on waistcoat or trousers. During 1947–48 a drape jacket became very popular; this was longer and more generous in cut, especially at the shoulders, hanging loose with little or no waist. Lapels were narrower with a changed line, sleeves tapered slightly towards the cuff, pockets were placed lower, and the Edwardian ticket pocket was revived. By 1949 the exaggerated drape was dying out and a more moderate cut with a softer, rounder shoulder-line and low waistline replaced it (Fig. 14). Jackets often had side-vents by 1949, and later some only a single vent at the back. Morning-coats with grey waistcoats continued to be worn on very formal occasions, though less frequently than before; this also applied to the evening coat, or 'tails', until some years after the Second World War. In 1953 the tails were cut square and lined with maroon silk; the collar was of velvet. The single-breasted dinner-jacket continued in favour, though by 1950 a double-breasted one was introduced (Fig. 3). Unlined lightweight jackets were sometimes worn in the summer. Corduroy jackets were fairly common for leisure wear in the middle of this period. A new proofed gaberdine was used for the zip-up jacket (Fig. 5). From 1931 lighter-weight zips were manufactured.

Matching waistcoats continued in use for more formal wear, but waistcoats of contrasting material and colour became very fashionable by 1950. For leisure an increasing number of pullovers, cardigans, and sweaters were worn in light- and later heavy-weight wools (Fig. 5).

Bolder colours were used much more for shirts during the fifties, also for socks, and particularly for ties. From 1950 jacket-style shirts in gay colours, hanging plain or belted, were often worn outside the trousers, jeans, or shorts (Fig. 7). Nylon was increasingly used for shirts from about 1954, though not on a wide scale.

Although during 1942 the Utility trousers were cut narrower and without turn-ups, the moderate width with turn-ups continued right through until the late forties (Figs. 1, 10), when trousers began to be cut increasingly narrower, tapering towards the ankle. Sometimes during the early fifties turn-ups were omitted; these narrower

George VI (1936-52) - Elizabeth II (1952-)

38 -46
1

42
2

'50
3

'55
4

5

'49
6

'50
7

8

9

10
1939-48

11
1948

12
1953

13
1955

14
1953-56

Drainpipe	'drainpipe' trousers were often of a darker cloth than the jacket, a fashion also followed in trousers of the more usual width. From 1949 there was a growing tendency for
Corduroy	tweed trousers matching the jacket, a two-piece country suit. During the earlier years
Zip-front	corduroys were often worn for leisure or by students. Grey worsteds usually had turn-ups;
Terylene	by about 1953 they too were more slimly tailored, with a new-style waistband, zip
worsted	front, two hip pockets, new colours, and crease-resisting cloth containing Terylene.
Overcoats	The darker tailored overcoat, single- or double-breasted, with set-in sleeve, continued

Drainpipe

Corduroy
Zip-front
Terylene
worsted
Overcoats

'drainpipe' trousers were often of a darker cloth than the jacket, a fashion also followed in trousers of the more usual width. From 1949 there was a growing tendency for tweed trousers matching the jacket, a two-piece country suit. During the earlier years corduroys were often worn for leisure or by students. Grey worsteds usually had turn-ups; by about 1953 they too were more slimly tailored, with a new-style waistband, zip front, two hip pockets, new colours, and crease-resisting cloth containing Terylene.

The darker tailored overcoat, single- or double-breasted, with set-in sleeve, continued as before, also the plain or belted raincoat. The tweed overcoat with raglan sleeve (p. 160, Fig. 7) remained popular throughout this period; from 1948 it was often made

Weatherproof cloth

in weatherproof cloth. By 1947-48 lapels and shoulders were cut more to the new style; during 1950 some coats were often shorter to above the knee, but the longer style of Fig. 13 was more usual for city wear by 1955. Velvet collars were introduced on these darker coats in 1950, sometimes with velvet cuffs as well. This tailored coat could be plain or half-belted at the back, a style also popular by 1955, in dark shower-proof gaberdine for city wear. These new proofed wool cloths or tweeds in many shades were worn a great deal for almost any style of coat, plain or belted (Fig. 8).

Zip-in linings
Reversible
Duffle coat
Hats

These all-weather coats could have detachable zip-in fleece or quilted linings, or some were made reversible: tweed with cotton gaberdine. Another popular coat during the fifties was the duffle coat, in camel, navy, or grey (Fig. 12).

There was a revival of the bowler from about 1949, also a new lightweight cap became popular; trilbies continued throughout this period.

Hair

The hair was still well trimmed at the back and sides, moustaches were less in evidence after about 1948. Teddy boys developed their own rather eccentric hair styles (Fig. 9), brushing the hair up and then forward.

Shoes

Leather shoes continued and, later, suède for less formal wear; soles were of leather, crêpe, and, later, nylon crêpe; sandals from the late forties, also 'slip-ons' or 'casuals', the latter and crêpe-soled shoes were much favoured by teddy boys.

Colours

Black jackets with striped trousers for formal wear, colours remained more sombre for city men; later, lighter shades of grey with an increase of browns tended to replace the darker shades. Waistcoats became much gayer; tweeds were brighter, with more use of fancy weaves. There were four shades of grey for worsteds by 1949, also many new colours, blue-grey, Lovat, browns, and, later, bronze. Black was still worn for evening dress, but midnight-blue was introduced in 1949 for both tails and dinner-jacket.

35

GEORGE VI (1936–52)

Women's Fashions: PART I (1936–47)

SKIRTS became short and shoulders square; the Second World War brought clothes-rationing and Utility garments; later the 'Asymmetrical' line appeared, followed by the 'New Look' in 1947.

The slender, tubular style continued until 1938 (Figs. 1, 2, 3), and waists remained *Dresses* normal; small waists and curves were accentuated in 1938 and again from 1946. Shoulders became increasingly square and padded during the Second World War (Figs. 9, 10), and the flat hips and trim, straight skirt gave women a far from feminine appearance. With the return to curves in 1946, attention was focused on waist and hips (Figs. 11, 12, 13), the Asymmetrical line was seen on dresses, suits, hats, and coats; *Asymmetrical* drapery, gathers, pleats, neckline, and hemline all playing their part (Fig. 12). The *line* neckline remained fairly high, especially for day, until 1944, when there was an increasing tendency for it to be cut lower, particularly for evening dress, where it was also cut wider (Fig. 7); sometimes, from 1946, only one shoulder was covered with drapery or strap; during that year Paris produced the 'off-the-shoulder' dress *Off-the-* (p. 175, Fig. 3); by 1947 the strapless evening dress had arrived, the bodice being finely *shoulder* boned to keep it in position (p. 178, Fig. 14), also a boned, strapless brassière was worn. *Strapless bra* A halter neckline seen on sun-tops or beach wear from about 1939 was also gaining in popularity (p. 175, Figs. 4, 7). Teenage American styles were fashionable, particularly one outfit consisting of matching or contrasting skirt, jacket, shirt, and sun-top, all being interchangeable and called 'separates'; in one form or another they could be worn *Separates* on any occasion. Improved zips were used in side-plackets. *Zip fasteners*

At first both long and short sleeves were fairly fitting to wrist or elbow and gathered *Sleeves* full on to the shoulder (Figs. 1, 2, 4, 5); later they were padded, giving an increasingly broad, square effect (Figs. 9, 10), until 1945, when less padding was used and the shoulder became more rounded (Fig. 12), becoming a sloping line by 1947 (Fig. 13). Until 1946 evening dresses had long or short sleeves, or, if they were sleeveless, a long- or short-sleeved matching bolero or jacket was frequently worn (Fig. 2).

Skirts became a little shorter each year on day dresses, until they reached to just *Skirt* below the knee in 1939 and from 1942–46 were short to the knee. Then, with a return to more graceful styles, an uncertain hemline was often longer to mid-calf (Fig. 12), preparing almost for the longer New Look introduced from Paris in the autumn of *The New* 1947 (Fig. 13 and p. 175, Fig. 10). Long evening dresses were usual (Figs. 2, 7), but *Look* during the Second World War some were made short to the knee. In 1937 there was an unsuccessful attempt to introduce an ankle-length or longer-at-the-back style, but it was not until 1946 that the uneven hemline became really fashionable for day or evening; this brought in the American-style ankle-length evening dress, which was to become popular during the fifties.

George VI (1936-52)
part I (1936-47)

1937 -38
1

'38 -45
2

'38 -39
3

4 '42

5 '42-46

A '40
6

'46 B

'46 C

D '46

E '46

F '40 -45

1946
7

'42-4
8

1942 -46
9

1942 -46
10

1946 -47
11

12
1946 -47

13
1947

Fabrics continued as before at first, with silk jersey greatly used in 1937. During and for some time after the Second World War supplies were short, quality decreased, and Utility cloth was introduced in 1942; rayon was much used. After 1946 many beautiful fabrics returned, Irish linens, tweeds, velvet, brocade, satin, lace, and silks.

Fitting coats remained fashionable (Fig. 9), also a three-quarter or hip length, hanging full, as in 1938 (Fig. 1), or straight and waistless from 1939 to 1946 (Fig. 3). The short, straight style was known as the 'box' jacket. Fitting jackets of contrasting colour were much worn during the Second World War (Fig. 10); boleros were fashionable. From 1946 tightly waisted coats reached to hip or mid-thigh (Fig. 11). Pockets were a prominent feature from 1942. Wide 'tent' coats were fashionable from 1941, especially a swing-back style of finger-tip length in 1941–42. Long-haired fur coats were seen until the Second World War (Fig. 1), half- to full-length. Hip-length evening fur capes were fashionable from 1946.

In 1938 hair was 'upswept' on top of the head (Fig. 2; compare p. 152, Fig. 3), in 1939 it was longer at the back as well, sometimes reaching the shoulders (Fig. 5, 6, 9). In 1940 it was dressed even higher on top, but was neater and more upswept off the face and neck by 1941 (Figs. 4, 6b, 8, 11, 12). The short American 'bubble cut' was introduced in 1946 (Fig. 7).

Hats were small, perched, usually, well forward, slightly over one eye. Veils, feathers, and ribbons were used a great deal, also fur until about 1940. In 1939 snoods of net, chenille, jersey, or velvet were worn with a pill-box hat, and a wider, flatter style completely covering the hair was seen in 1943. By 1942 hats were often larger, with a wide, upward-curved brim. Many close-fitting 'off-the-face' new styles were worn from 1946. Coloured scarves, tied turban-fashion (Fig. 6f), were common from 1940, but by 1943–46 tying under the chin was more usual (Fig. 9).

In 1938 summer shoes were often made with a 'wedge' sole, some with a 'sling-back' heel (Fig. 5); later these soles were made higher at the back, forming a wedge heel (Fig. 8). Practical, low-heeled shoes and sandals dominated the Second World War years; from 1940 many showed a Dutch influence (Fig. 9), when wooden soles were introduced; leather and crêpe (Fig. 10) were also used. From 1944 ankle-strap styles were seen, and higher heels began to return. The built-up 'platform' sole became increasingly popular, particularly on a sling-back 'peep-toe' shoe (Fig. 12), or with ankle strap and cut-out toe and heel (p. 175, Fig. 10). Fleece-lined bootees were introduced about 1940.

Rayon stockings were usual; nylon ones were not generally obtainable until the last year or two of this period.

From 1940 'slacks' were worn for work, during air-raids, or for leisure (Fig. 8).

Handbags with a shoulder strap were fashionable from 1942 to 1946 (Fig. 10), otherwise plain narrow ones were carried at first (Figs. 1, 5); later various styles as shown in Figs. 3, 12 were more popular.

Jewellery was large and 'showy' in 1938; chunky 'gold' neckbands or lengths of 'gold' chain were worn round neck and wrist in 1945.

Black continued fashionable, with white accessories from 1940; black, white, and many pastel shades for evenings except during the Second World War, when all colours were harsher and brighter. Also navy blue for spring, browns, greens, and wine colours for autumn, red (popular for accessories in 1939), snuff, ice-blue, and maize.

Materials
Silk jersey
Utility cloth
Rayon
Coats

Box jacket

Tent coats

Hair

Bubble cut

Hats

Head-scarves

Shoes
Wedge

Wood and
  crêpe soles
Platform sole
Peep-toe shoe
Snow-boots

Stockings

Slacks
Handbags

Jewellery

Colours

173

GEORGE VI (1936–52)

Women's Fashions : PART II (1947–52)

THE New Look was followed by a period of contrasts, with fashions for all ages and all figures. Hair was cut short again; there was an increasing use of nylon.

Dresses
The New Look

The near-ankle-length hemline, bouffant skirts, tiny waist, padded hips, and sloping shoulder-line of the New Look of 1947 (Fig. 10) were more modified by 1948. Spring 1949 brought in the flying-panel period (Fig. 11), with panels back, front,

Flying panels

or side, longer or shorter than the sheath-style dress. For evening wear the panels were long and the skirt was shorter and often slit. Sheath dresses were very popular

Sheath

by 1950 (Fig. 12); buttons were an important feature, and also bows; pockets were large and pouched or with flaps, pointed, stiffened, or jutting; they were breast-high or on the hips, or both. The Asymmetrical line continued (Fig. 2) with hips or shoulders swathed or draped, with fullness at back or side, made by gathers, pleats, or flares (p. 178, Fig. 14). From 1948 the neckline could be deeply pointed or draped to one side; it was cut lower (Fig. 11), either square or narrow, heart-shaped or scooped ; for evening it was wide and low or off-the-shoulder; the halter neckline continued (Figs. 4, 7, 9). Waists remained tiny; 1950 saw more emphasis on the hips. Many dresses had a higher waistline from 1951.

Sleeves

Three-quarter-length sleeves remained very fashionable; long sleeves were wide and loose or sometimes tapered to a fitting cuff. By 1950 summer dresses were sleeveless or had tiny cap sleeves and often had matching boleros (Fig. 6). The sloped, or dropped, shoulder-line was emphasized by the 'raglan' or 'dolman' style (Figs. 2, 11, 12, 13).

Skirt
Dirndl

Both the full skirt with stiffly frilled petticoats and the pencil-slim skirt were most fashionable for day and evening. The young American-style dirndl (Fig. 8) was very popular from 1950, and the American-style ballet-length evening dress (Fig. 4) was seen more frequently.

Knitwear

Woollen jumpers worn from the early thirties, sometimes with a cardigan to match, gained in popularity, in spite of the wool shortage from 1939 to 1945, until

Twin-set

by 1946 the 'twin-set' (Fig. 5) had become extremely fashionable: a 'must' for every woman's wardrobe.

Fabrics

Many more woollens were used, especially tweeds and worsteds, for dresses from 1951. There was a revival of silks, organdie, chiffon, lace, and of soft fabrics over stiff petticoats; also taffeta, faille, moiré, stiff satin, velvet, jersey, and rayon; metal-thread

Spot-proof
and Nylon

brocades in 1951 and spot-proof cotton and velvet. Nylon, used in the national war effort, was now usual for stockings, underwear, and blouses.

Coats

Besides the fitting coat (p. 172, Fig. 13), the full, tent coat became very fashionable (Fig. 13), particularly with a high or cape collar and swing-back effect, until 1950, when a three-quarter-length was worn. Button-on capes were popular. In 1947 and

174

George VI (1936-52)
part II (1947-52)

1950
1

1950
2

3

1949
evening
dress

4
1951
dance
dress

5

1949
6

1947
7

1951
8

1951
9

10
1947

11
1949-50

12
1951

13
1948-50

from 1950 a narrow, waistless, straight-hanging coat returned to favour, of cloth or tweed or made to match the dress. From 1949 coatings were heavy, of a deep, thick pile or rough-textured surface. Linings were gay and coats made reversible (p. 178, Fig. 11), plain with plaid or colour. Fur trimmings were used more from 1950. All-weather coats of proofed gaberdine, fine corduroy, or velvet were worn, many with a matching hood (Fig. 1). A 'duster' coat was introduced in 1951 (p. 178, Fig. 4), at first of black taffeta, later also of dupion, in pale pastel shades; it was often reversible in two colours, and, made weatherproof with matching hat, it could be worn as a raincoat, summer coat, or evening wrap. There were many styles of jackets, from the tight-waisted (Fig. 10), the slender (Fig. 2), and the tailored (Fig. 13), to the straight-hanging box or tiny boleros so popular during the fifties. From 1948 huge scarves, or 'stoles', were extremely fashionable for day or evening (Figs. 3, 4); they were of fur or almost any fabric from wool to fine lace or net.

By autumn 1948 hair became shorter, following American influence, then in 1949 the 'urchin' cut appeared (Fig. 11), and many short styles followed (Figs. 3, 4, 7). Long hair also returned to favour, worn in a huge coil on top or at the back of the head (Fig. 12). Many teen-agers wore their hair long in a 'pony-tail' (Fig. 8).

Various forms of a type of 'cloche' hat were fashionable (Figs. 10, 13), also tiny skullcaps, often of feathers (p. 178, Fig. 13), 'beanies', and helmets. From about 1949 there was a distinct forward movement, with many large hats spreading out at front or sides. By 1950 both large and small hats were worn straight (Figs. 2, 12), the small ones in particular often dipping at the sides.

The year 1949 saw the end of the ankle-strap, open-heel and peep-toe shoe (Fig. 10). Afternoon shoes were dainty (Fig. 11), sometimes of fine interlaced straps, a style most fashionable for evenings (Fig. 3); heels were medium to high; low heels were usual for walking; heelless pumps (Fig. 8, 9) or shoes with inch-high Cuban heels were worn during the fifties; and the popularity of the suède or leather snow-boot was increasing (Fig. 1).

American-style 'jeans' were commonly seen on teen-agers, but many women used them for caravan, leisure, or holiday wear (Fig. 9). Although the 1947 Continental 'bikini' created rather a sensation, a more modified bathing two-piece was a little more usual here (Fig. 7).

More elaborate necklaces and earrings were worn with the new short hair styles (Fig. 3); several rows of pearls were fashionable, also chunky 'gold' jewellery in 1951.

Brown was in favour, from pale snuff to near black, for day or evening, with greys and pinks for summer. Very dark shades of browns and greens were worn in the autumn. An apricot-orange shade was popular in 1950, also blue. White was used a great deal for everything from 1950, and black for accessories. Evening shades were delicate, two colours often being used together on a dress.

Reversible
Weather-
proof
Duster

Jackets

Stoles

Hair
Urchin cut

Pony-tail
Hats

Shoes

Snow-boot

Jeans

Bikini

Jewellery

Colours

36

ELIZABETH II (1952–　)

Women's Fashions: PART I (1952-56)

WAISTS were high, low, or natural with slender sheath dresses or wide, full skirts; the shorter evening hemline was more generally accepted; fabrics were improved.

Although the waistline was a 'wandering' one, it was slender (Fig. 13), sometimes with the emphasis high (Fig. 16), or low (Fig. 14), or both (Fig. 15), having a smooth bust-to-hip effect, though the low-waisted 'beetle-back' line from Paris in 1953 was an exception to this; by 1955 half-belts worn low at the back were increasingly used on dresses, suits (Fig. 12), and coats; the Paris 'A' line was also much favoured then. Necklines were often draped (Fig. 3) and were high, medium, or low (Fig. 13). Evening dresses usually had the shoulders covered or had narrow straps—1953–55. The general silhouette was neater from 1954. | Dresses

The set-in, slender sleeve helped much with the neater effect (Figs. 13, 16) as opposed to the raglan or dolman sleeve (Fig. 9). Wrist-length or tiny cap sleeves (Fig. 10) were fashionable, also the three-quarter length as before. | Sleeves

The length of the sheath or bouffant skirt varied from about eleven and a quarter inches to the London length of thirteen and a half inches from the ground. Long evening gowns, full-skirted or sheath, were fashionable in 1954; in 1953 and 1955 the slender dresses were sometimes flared out trumpet-fashion from below the knee, following a 1950 style. The shorter day-length evening gown was very popular by 1955. The hip-line was often draped on day (Fig. 6b) or evening dresses; permanently pleated skirts were worn for any occasion (Figs. 4, 9). | Skirts *Permanently pleated*

Striped patterns and flowery prints were fashionable in 1952, also linens, shantung, silk crêpe, cottons, rayon, wool jersey, Irish linens, and tweeds—tweeds for dresses from 1954 (Fig. 16). Nylon, Terylene, and wool-like, moth-proof Orlon from 1953, were all crease-resisting and had no ironing and permanent pleating qualities, also Tricel in 1956. Most fabrics, including wool, rayon, and nylon, could be made water-repellent, shrink-proof, and crease-resistant by 1953. The softer fabrics were used more (1953–56) for day and evening, also velvet, faille, lamé, heavy lace, satin, and tulle. Very rich fabrics were worn for evenings in 1954, also much delicate and rich embroidery. A petticoat of stiff felt was sometimes worn under the full skirt in 1953, replacing several petticoats. By 1955 wide, coloured felt skirts, gathered or flared, and later patterned, were worn with the sweater. | Fabrics *Moth-proof Crease-resisting No ironing Water-repellent Shrink-proof*

The Italian sweater revival with the use of heavy wools gave a bulky appearance to their hip-length styles so popular from 1954 (Fig. 5). Fine-quality wools were also used a great deal (Figs. 9, 11) and twin-sets were as fashionable as ever; during this period the cardigan was frequently worn buttoning down the back. | Knitwear

The straight coat continued for summer or winter wear (Fig. 11); but 1953 saw | Coats

Elizabeth II (1952 -)

'52
2

'55
3

5

'54
A 6 B

'53

7

'53-56
8   9

'52
-54
1

'51
-56
4

10 '53
    -56

11

'51
-55

'55
-56
12

1952
13

evening
dress

14

1953-56
15
afternoon
or
dance dress

1956
16

a return of the tent coat with a wide hemline, also coats of all lengths from half to near full length, and these, by 1955, tended to be cut narrower, while the tent coat became wider. Weather-proof coats with matching hat were worn a great deal (Fig. 2). Many dresses, particularly those with a low neckline, often had matching boleros (Fig. 6b), jackets or coats forming two-piece outfits, which were very popular from 1955. Duster coats were worn as before (Fig. 4), also a very lightweight mackintosh in a new synthetic fabric. Winter coats remained bulky. Fur linings were more usual than fur coats, though there was a return of these by 1956 with shorter-haired furs being used. Fur and a much-improved nylon fur fabric were used a great deal for collars, cuffs (Fig. 1), muffs, tippets, and even hats in 1955–56. Fur or fabric stoles continued most fashionable (Fig. 16), also fur capes for evenings. Short duffle coats in camel, white, navy, or grey were often worn by teen-agers (Fig. 8). *Two-piece*

Nylon fur fabric Stoles *Duffle coats*

The short haircut showed Italian influence; longer styles were also fashionable by 1954 (Fig. 15). Hair

Very small hats were favoured, either cloche-shaped, entirely covering the hair, or set flat on top of the head; also wide, flat 'tray' or inverted-bowl shapes were popular (Figs. 6b, 10). Hats

Delicate sandals, often with very high heels, were worn for day or evening; also many low-cut pumps. Towards 1955 a dainty shoe with a much more pointed toe became fashionable; the 'Louis' heels were either medium, low, or very tiny (Figs. 12, 16). Shoes

Jeans continued as before, usually of near-ankle length; black, coloured, or tartan, they tended to replace the dirndl skirt as casual wear for teen-agers (Fig. 8). Jeans

One-piece strapless bathing-dresses were more usual during this period (Fig. 7); Italian fashions had a strong influence over beach and other casual wear. Bathing-dress

Much artificial jewellery was worn, buckles, clasps, and multi-twists of beads and semi-precious stones, also large paste clips and earrings. Jewellery

Pale, creamy colours were very popular, blonde, sherry, and beiges from string to beaver; as a contrast there were many new rich colours in 1953, gay and brilliant. Yellows, blues, violet and lilac, and especially pinks, were worn, also many shades of browns and greens, as well as charcoal, steel, and black. Colours

ELIZABETH II (1952-   )

Men's Fashions : PART II (1956-68)

URING the 1960's Englishmen became increasingly fashion-conscious. There was a new, slim-cut line to a higher-fastening, flared jacket with waisted styling and a drift towards two-piece suits which could be worn for town or country. There were short car coats, leather coats and fur hats, and a wide range of casuals and co-ordinates, ranging from the more conservative clothes to the 'way-out' Carnaby Street gear for the teen-ager. The 'teddy boys' gave way to the 'beatniks' and the 'mods' and 'rockers' of the early sixties, and to the 'hippies' of these last two years. Beards returned, after being out of favour for half a century, and longer hair styles were seen on the young.

Coat or jacket — Formal suits remained conventional at first, with S.B. (single-breasted) two-button-style jacket, giving way by 1961 to the three-button fastening (Figs. 16, 19), with natural shoulder-line and narrow lapels, being slightly waisted and lengthened with a slimmer, closer fit. From 1964 the waist emphasis increased, and in 1966 the new trend was towards a low waist with longer, flared jacket and ten-inch side-vents, slanting flapped pockets and flared cuffs (Fig. 17), or a long, centre back-vent was used with the flapped pockets set straight or slanting (Plate VIII). By 1966 D.B. (double-breasted) styles were also popular (Fig. 20); there was a 'high' look with four-button S.B. fastening (Fig. 14), some of the latter, by 1968, with collar but no lapels, and by the autumn, for formal or casual wear, a plain style appeared with concealed button-fastening and simple stand collar.

Cardigan jacket — In 1958 a new Italian-style cardigan jacket was introduced for leisure wear, in plain or striped light-weight woollen cloth or all-wool jersey-knit. It had no collar or lapels or top pocket. From 1962 it became increasingly popular (Fig. 18). The cardigan in one form or another now often replaced the tweed jacket for casual wear; made in fine or heavy rib-knit (Fig. 15) in wool, wool-and-nylon mixture, or Bri-nylon, with raglan or set-in sleeve, it sometimes had front panels of tweed, suède, or leather (Fig. 9). In 1961 an all-tweed sweater jacket was designed on similar lines, with collar and raglan sleeves, to be worn over bulky sweaters. From the sixties a variety of military-style coats were sold in Carnaby Street.

Jersey-knit Cardigan

Bri-nylon Sweater jacket

Military coats

Evening dress Linen tuxedo — The dark dinner-suit of black barathea with silk lapel continued, but was replaced for summer wear in 1958 by an Irish linen tuxedo with wide shawl collar (Fig. 1); it was also made in Terylene. By the sixties a narrow shawl collar of ribbed silk was usual on the S.B. dark dinner-jacket (Fig. 13), and a wide cummerbund was sometimes worn. From 1958 there was a definite attempt to introduce more colour, and a mulberry-toned evening suit was designed with Burgundy-satin collar and buttons. It was worn with a

Lace cravat — frilled lace cravat and cuffs and pintucked shirts. Some light summer evening suits were made entirely of Terylene by 1966, similar in cut to Fig. 19, but without the ticket

180

Elizabeth II (1952-)
part II ('56-'68)

pocket or flap to breast pocket. On full evening suits, seen now less frequently, the tails were slightly longer and narrower; also the silk lapels were narrower than before.

From 1961 morning suits for formal occasions sometimes had grey or check trousers, or, for summer wear, fine grey suiting was used for the entire suit.

Some trousers still had turn-ups at first (Fig. 5), but by late 1961 these were usually omitted. The cut was slim and tapering, with permanent crease and plain front with a single or, later, no waist pleat; some were very form-fitting. The zip fastener was used. The flare line, first launched in 1958, was not successful here, although by 1966 there was a definite, subtle flare outward, as in Fig. 17. Hippies wore an exaggerated flared trouser (Fig. 2); jeans were still worn by students, teen-agers (Fig. 3), and long-haired beatniks. Shorts for sport and holiday wear were very brief. Hipster trousers, often in checks (Fig. 12), were popular in the mid-sixties.

For town wear, suitings in close, fine cloths had an increasing trend towards stripes (Figs. 16, 20), varying from hair-line effects to bold multi-weaves, with a greater range of colour, which was even more noticeable in tweeds for leisure wear (Fig. 17), plain
or in stronger checks, in a wide range of weights, textures, and weaves. Drip-dry Terylene polyester fibre was used alone, or in wool mixtures, or, from 1958, with linen, for summer lightweight suits and unlined jackets. Corduroy velvet in fine or wide
stripe continued for casual wear (Fig. 14), also, from the mid-sixties, brown leather or suède coats, tailored as in Fig. 16. Black leather 'battledress' jackets (Fig. 12) were favoured by the rockers. This style was also worn by teenagers in corduroy or nylon. Weatherproof button-up or zip-up jackets or anoraks (similar to Fig. 5, p. 169) of plain or quilted Bri-nylon were popular for holiday or casual wear. Some young mods in 1963–64 were still wearing the American-style Madras cotton jacket (Fig. 3), although in 1964 the more dressy suit (Fig. 19) was more typical of this adolescent style. Flower- patterned jackets were often worn by hippies (Fig. 2), who in winter fancied rough fur waistcoats.

Thick, chunky-knit sweaters with V, rounded 'crew' neck or popular polo style (Figs. 10, 14, and Plate VIII) were increasingly fashionable for leisure wear from 1958; also, from 1963, the thick, richly patterned Aran sweaters. Other hip-length pullovers, with or without sleeves, were also made in finer knitwear of wools, Shetlands, and cashmeres. Striped sweaters became popular from 1966 (Fig. 4).

Matching and contrasting waistcoats continued, but one in tailored knitwear, with rib-knitted front and sateen-lined pockets, was worn a great deal.

By 1962 shirts were far more colourful, plain, checked, or striped, of drip-dry cottons, finest wool yarns, or Bri-nylon. Sometimes dark shirts were worn with a lighter tie (Fig. 11); button-down collars were seen from the mid-sixties (Figs. 12, 19). There was a very wide range of sports shirts in all shades and colours (Fig. 15), with long or short sleeves, usually of drip-dry, non-iron material. Recently a new line of shirt, with plain round standing collar, was introduced, of silk or satin for evening wear. Ties were far more colourful, some horizontally striped, woven or knitted, or Paisley patterned.

The wide range of overcoats varied in length from knee to hip-level, but by 1961 the shorter styles (Fig. 7) were popular, particularly the car coat (Fig. 6) and the fleece-lined suède coat (Fig. 10). The storm-proof cloth or tweed coat (Fig. 11) and the insulated weatherproof coat with plaid lining, of 1958 (Fig. 5), remained favourites, but were shorter in length before 1968. A two-tone reversible shower-proof coat appeared in the mid-sixties. Many tweed coats were foam-backed and weather-resistant (Figs. 7, 8), and fur collars were popular. Fur pile fabrics in Acrilan or Orlon were used for some car coats (Figs. 6) or for linings from 1962. *Foam-backed* *Fur* and *fur* *pile*

Rough-textured, tweed or corduroy hats were common in the sixties (Figs. 6, 11), with crowns tapered and brims narrower, some Tyrolean styles being extremely so. Caps continued (Figs. 5, 9) being narrower in the sixties. The curly-brimmed bowler (Fig. 8), usually black, was sometimes made in grey or brown. By winter 1964 the fur Cossack hat (Fig. 7) was increasingly popular, made in sealskin, beaver, black Persian lamb, or white lamb's wool. *Hats* *Tyrolean* *Cossack*

Younger men favoured a longer hair style by 1960 (Figs. 10, 11, 15, 17); some wore beards (Fig. 18), often with a droopy moustache as well (Fig. 4); others fancied a neatly pointed beard or even a large, bushy variety. During 1963 the Beatles' long haircut (Fig. 13), then considered eccentric, influenced men's hair styles considerably, and the American close-cropped look of 1963 (Fig. 3) was soon replaced by the long brushed-forward fringed style with sideboards (Figs. 4, 12, 14, 19, 20). The extremely long-haired, untidy, bearded beatniks were comparable to the hippies of the later sixties (Fig. 2), who often had a piled-up, frizzed mop of hair. More conventional hair styles continued. The droopy moustache, without a beard, was frequently seen by 1968. *Hair* *Beatles* *Beatniks* *Hippies*

The 1958 Italian-style 'feather-light' and 'glove-like' fitting shoe, of suède or calf, with lightweight leather or cushioned rubber sole, was popular (Fig. 15), also lightweight, stain-proof, and water-repellent suèdes (Fig. 17). Besides traditional lace-ups (Fig. 16), various casual styles were worn (Fig. 18), also the plain, elastic-sided shoe (Fig. 21b). From 1963 young men and teen-agers often wore elastic-sided, high ankle-boots with a higher heel than usual (Fig. 21d), and this Cuban heel on shoe or boot was popular with the slim-fitting tapered trouser (Fig. 12). The extremely pointed 'winkle-picker' of the early sixties (Fig. 21a) was more usual among young city dwellers, and was comparable with the women's shoes of that time. Ankle-high suède 'safari' boots, with crêpe soles and flatter heel, were popular for casual wear from c. 1965 (Fig. 21e and Plate VIII), as were also the canvas shoe (Fig. 21c) and the basket shoe (Fig. 3). *Shoes* *Water-repellent suède* *Cuban heel* *Winkle-picker* *Safari boots*

By 1961 pure wool and nylon socks were much more brightly coloured, plain, striped, or patterned, and were self-supporting, being made with Lastex yarn throughout the calf ribbing or ankle ribbing on the shorter socks. *Socks* *Self-supporting*

Sun-glasses were increasingly worn as an affectation rather than a necessity (Fig. 4), and during the sixties this applied also to spectacles, particularly among some teenagers who fancied a round, rimless variety; the girls' ones were often tinted. *Spectacles*

Drabness in men's clothes was gradually ousted by brighter, richer colours and more striking tweeds. Black and greys, with charcoal and dark blues, still headed the list for town-wear suitings, but by 1968 brown had become increasingly fashionable as a basic colour, with an infinite variety of blends and shades from beige to cognac, also greens from moss to olive. There were two-tone effects, such as copper bronze with black, with various types of stripes being most popular, with stronger checks and tweeds for casual wear by 1966, and with summer suits and jackets in pale greys and fawns. Co-ordinate colour ranges were introduced for jackets, trousers, sweaters, and hats. Dark shades of green, maroon, or blue were used for dinner-jackets from 1961. During the later sixties youths fancied 'gay' uniforms of the past or 'flower-power' shirts and jackets. Leisure shirts and holiday wear were bright, striped, checked, or patterned. *Colours*

183

ELIZABETH II (1952-   )

Women's Fashions: PART II (1956-63)

DURING 1957 there was a re-emergence of 'legs', and nearly every woman shortened her skirts during 1958, although the hemline remained below knee-level. Adolescent styles had a marked effect on fashions, and by 1961 there were many outfits available which looked equally well on mother and daughter. Dual-purpose clothes, suitable for day or evening wear, were popular, and the afternoon dress virtually disappeared. Teen-agers wore chunky sweaters with tight trousers, or with skirts and coloured stockings. Waistlines were high, low, or normal, most women went hatless, and hair styles became higher and higher. Wigs and false-hair pieces were sold in the shops, and stiletto heels ruined many a floor surface.

Dresses
Sack
Drip-dry
Jersey

The plain straight 'sack' from Paris in 1957, although not accepted in England, left its effect on the popular sheath-line, with its slim skirt, incurved front, and often dipping, rounded back. The permanently pleated, drip-dry Tricel dress, although here belted (Fig. 4), shows this influence. This finely pleated, silky-looking jersey was not hemmed, but could usefully be cut to any length; with shortening skirts, two inches were cut off in 1960, and by 1961 kneecap-level was reached on some dresses.

Trapeze
Baby doll

Shirt-waister

Bell skirt

In 1958 the 'trapeze' line (Fig. 5) and the 'baby-doll' look both helped to popularize shorter skirts and gave the extremely short, off-the-ground length that year of twenty inches! Full-skirted, button-through dresses were very fashionable from 1957, but the square or rounded neckline was generally replaced by a shirt-waisted style in 1958 (Fig. 14); made as a dress, or separate top and skirt, with a sewn-in, stiffened petticoat, this was a best-seller in 1959, when it was almost impossible to find the slim, straight style preferred by older women (Fig. 12). Other tapering bell-skirted fashions appeared for day or evening wear, long or short (Fig. 1), with overskirt as here, or with single skirt worn over its frilled petticoat, shaped to the wide hip-line. The years 1959–61 were those of contrasts: both full- and slim-skirted dresses appeared side by side.

Empire line

Evening
dress

Permanently box-pleated skirts were fashionable in 1961 and 1962 on the slim, straight styles in crease-resistant material (Fig. 3). Some fully pleated dresses had a wide plain waistband, giving a high Empire line, seen also on the long evening dresses; these were either full- or slim-skirted, or a mixture of both (Fig. 6). The slender, high-waisted evening dress remained popular up to 1968, usually sleeveless, although long sleeves were worn from 1961 to 1964. Short evening dresses also stayed in fashion, full-skirted, in 1958–62, or slim; some, of softly draped chiffon (Fig. 2), could also be full-length.

Shift
Two-piece
Sleeveless
dress

Straight, sleeveless shift dresses, many with a matching jacket (Fig. 17), continued into 1968, plain or patterned, with high waistline from 1958, or belted at normal or hip level, or not belted at all. Vertically striped sleeveless dresses of Indian cottons, or silks, were popular in 1961, otherwise large floral prints, particularly of roses, were seen a great deal. In 1962 some sleeveless dresses had a four-inch pleated frill at the knee,

184

Elizabeth II (1952–)
part II (1956–63)

1
2
3
4
5
6   1958
7
8
9
10
11

'58 –'62

'59 –'62

'61 –'62

'59 60

1959

'61   from '62   from '57   1963   '61

'58 –'60

59 63

2

13
from
1959

14

15
1961–63

16
1961

17

18

1960 –'62

a 19
'61
b
c   '63

Tunic dress giving a rising, uncertain look to the hemline, an effect also found in the sleeved tunic dress of 1959–67, when the overskirt was short to well above the knee, with the slim underskirt showing below, a fashion liked by older women.

Sack-back The influence of the 1957 'sack' dress, which eventually killed the 1947 'New Look', was found in another style seen for a few years from 1958. This dress, for day or evening wear, short or full length, had a figure-fitting front, but the back hung loose in a straight fall from neck to hem; it could be made of draped chiffon, as in Fig. 2, or of a silk or satin for evening, when sometimes the front was embroidered.

Sweater dress From 1961 the sweater dress, knit plain or in rib, with long sleeves and high neckline (Fig. 16), completely ousted the once popular shirt-waister. Plain or with tie-belt at waist or hip-level, it was considered short, barely covering the knees. By 1963–64 it was made in various ribs, textures, and colours. Also from 1961, teen-agers fancied the *Leather shift* sleeveless leather shift (Fig. 15), either in suède or in coloured nappa lamb. Some wore *Suède* a waistcoat and skirt style; or a hip-length tunic of black leather, fringed at the hem, was worn with tight trousers and knee-high boots from 1962 by the 'ton-up kids' and 'rockers'.

Sleeves The three-quarter-length sleeve, seen since 1947, was losing its popularity towards 1961, when longer sleeves returned, although these on knitwear were often pushed up, still giving the three-quarter look. Tiny cap sleeves were usual on summer or evening dresses, but shoulders were less covered during the sixties.

Skirts Permanently pleated full skirts continued up to *c.* 1960, when pleated reversible *Reversible* tartan skirts were popular for a short while. The full skirt on self-supporting petticoat, so popular in 1958 and 1959, gave way to the ever-shortening pencil-slim skirt from 1959. From 1960 a knee-length, slightly flared skirt was seen for two years, and from 1961 to 1964 some slim skirts had inverted pleats back and front (Fig. 10) or a single pleat at the back (Fig. 9). From 1962 the blouse or sweater was often darker in colour than the skirt.

Knitwear The button-through cardigan twin-set changed little; made in fine wools, Orlon, *Courtelle* Courtelle, Bri-lon, or mixtures of these, it was still liked, particularly by older women. *Bri-lon* Teen-agers preferred chunky-knit sweaters (Fig. 13), in double-knit wools, soft brushed *Chunky knit* mohair, or quick-dry Orlon; often they borrowed from their menfolk's wardrobes. Hip-length or longer, they were worn with skirt or trousers, the high polo-neck style often being a feature from 1960, worn with a collarless jacket or coat.

Coats Full-length coats were loose-fitting and easy, often with a shawl collar (Fig. 17). A wide-spreading tent coat continued into 1961, but straighter coats, sometimes collarless, were worn from 1958; from 1960 a wide-set, upstanding collar became increasingly fashionable (p. 191, Fig. 2). Some straight coats, tapering in to the knee, were of three-*Sheepskin* quarter length, and a low-set half-belt was seen up to 1961 (Fig. 11). Suède sheepskin coats became more popular each year (Fig. 10), and from 1961 were made in ten different shades in soft browns to greens.

During the sixties wide tent styles and later slim tailored full-length coats were worn with the long evening dress, often in matching material; fur stoles remained fashionable, also fur jackets from 1959.

Fur From 1962 fur trimmings were used with everything, on wraps, coats, jackets, and hats—some furs, such as fox, being dyed even apricot or green in order to match suit or coat.

186

Nylon, once a miracle fabric, was now commonplace, and man-made fibres in increasing variety gave a very wide range of materials, plain or as mixtures, with nylon, Orlon, and others as before. From 1959 Bri-lon and Ban-lon, and since 1960 many Acrilan fabrics with 'easy care' properties, and like brushed nylon, gave soft suèdes, and could be mixed with wool or rayon. Also from 1960, stretch fabrics, such as Crimplene (pure Terylene), were ideal for dresses or swim-wear; there were elastic knitted fabrics for cuffs and welts, and stretch denim for trousers (Fig. 8); from 1961 stretch nylon with rayon, and woven Bri-nylon stretch fabrics; also that year bonded foam-backed materials, in wool, cotton, or man-made fibres, gave insulation against heat or cold; they had bulk, warmth, softness, and lightness, and were invaluable for coats or interlinings. By 1962 Courtelle was improved; looking and feeling like wool, it was made in a wide range of weights, textures, and mixtures, in pastel or vivid colours, from fine silky fabrics to heavy knits and tweeds. *[margin: Fabrics / Ban-lon / Acrilan / Stretch fabrics / Crimplene / Bri-nylon / Foam-backed / Insulation / Courtelle]*

More softly draping, often sheer materials were used from 1962, and crêpes from 1963.

From September 1959 woollen fabrics were made with drip-dry, non-iron qualities the same as synthetics. Jersey-knit, growing in favour since 1955, became a real fashion fabric from 1958, when, as a double-knit, it was made in England in any material from man-made fibres to silk and wool, and even a tweed jersey in 1961. Also that year, for evening wear, there was a drip-dry Ban-lon Lurex jersey, a most fashionable 'glitter' fabric made with metallic yarns. *[margin: Drip-dry wools / Jersey double-knit / Metallic yarns]*

From 1960 crisp, crease-resistant cottons were given a sheen or satin finish, and, like linens, were even more crease-resistant and drip-dry, as were also new colourful gaberdines for coats, skirts, and slacks, being washable and shrink-proof. In 1962 new proofed nylon was on sale for holiday wear and boating, lightweight anoraks (Fig. 8), plain or quilted, also over-trousers. Another weatherproof and water-repellent fabric used for rain-wear from 1962 was PVC, a very shiny, thin Polyvinyl plastic sheeting, the seams being welded or sewn; by 1966 this was most popular among teen-agers, particularly in black or red, cut similar to Fig. 7, p. 191, plain or banded horizontally in contrasting colours, and sometimes with patch pockets. Traditional, lovely coloured tweeds continued fashionable, with small checks popular in 1960, and from 1961 to 1963 more open chunky curl coatings, with black curl on strongly contrasting grounds, were seen everywhere. By 1963 closer fine weaves returned; sometimes different-looking cloths were worn together, making a matching outfit. From 1961 there were corduroys in needle-cord to wide rib, also long- or short-pile fabrics knitted or woven in wool, nylon, or other blends, for coats, jackets, or linings. Pure silks or silk-and-nylon mixtures were fashionable, also chiffon, velvet, or stiff brocades for evening wear and formal occasions. *[margin: Proofed nylon / PVC / Tweeds / Pile fabrics]*

By 1960 zip or slide fasteners of plastic nylon filament were made in a very wide range of colours, the filament, tape, and thread being dyed together; small, feather-light, and flexible, they were used on finest wools or fabrics. Most dresses now fastened down centre-back, from neck to below waist-level. Press fasteners for plastic or leather-wear goods were made with tops in widest range of colours or with metallic finish. From 1962 a new Bri-nylon touch-and-close press strip fastening, Velcro, was used for closing waist-, wrist-, or ankle-bands on play suits, holiday or casual wear, and other items. *[margin: Fasteners / Zips in colour / Press / Touch and close / Holiday wear]*

Fitting trews or slacks continued (Figs. 8, 18), with increasing use of gayer colours

187

or tartans. Some easy-fitting, hip-length summer-wear tops were of vertical or horizontal Mexican-style striped prints in 1959–60, with Madras striped cottons being more popular from 1961; also short tops were worn with wide, bell-bottomed trousers (Fig. 7), which were a little reminiscent of the beach pyjamas of the early thirties. Stripes were also used on some one-piece bathing-suits and on the very brief bikinis from 1963.

Various short and longer hair styles continued, some with a brushed-forward look (Figs. 2, 14, and p. 178, Fig. 15), but by 1959 there was a definite increase in height

obtained by back combing (Figs. 4, 10, 11), with a fashion among younger women for the curled outward style (Fig. 13), or forward with a fringe from 1961 (Figs. 9, 15). The

high, narrow, back-combed 'beehive' style (Figs. 1, 6, 16, 18) was often aided by lacquer, wigs, or false-hair switches from early in the sixties, when a new permanent wave was devised giving a springy resilience to the roots only, leaving the rest of the hair 'fluid'. From 1961 the hair was sometimes drawn up into a bun or coil (Fig. 3), or held by a ribbon band to which a switch was attached (Figs. 7, 8). Pageboy 'bobs'

outmoded the exaggerated beehive style by 1963. From 1961 dark make-up outlined the eyes, and lips were pale or very pale.

Hats, occasionally worn with the rising hair styles, became higher in the crown and were set flat on the head (Fig. 17); from 1958 there were some upturned brims (Fig. 5), and inverted-bowl shapes from 1959, when flower-covered hats appeared (Fig. 12) and remained popular; also feather and fur hats, and from 1962 high-built turbans.

Elegant, low-cut shoes, often in gay or light colours, appeared with the shorter skirts. By 1959 toes were 'arrow-pointed' (Figs. 3, 4) with stiletto heels. Low-heeled casuals (Fig. 8) or pumps (Figs. 7, 18) were for leisure wear. In 1960 a 'crop-toed' shoe

was seen in Paris and Italy, and by autumn 1961 the chisel toe with small curved heel (Figs. 11, 16, 19*a* and *b*) brought an end to the now vulgar 'winkle-picker' (Fig. 13). Slightly rounded toes with Cuban heels appeared by 1963 (Fig. 19*c*). Ankle- and near-

calf-length boots, but by 1962 and 1963 higher, zip-fastened fitting boots in leather or suède, reaching to just below the knee, were fashionable winter wear (Fig. 9). Black leather boots were popular then among teen-agers for everyday use except in summer.

Flesh-coloured seamed nylon stockings continued (Fig. 11), but from 1960 seam-free mesh stockings, made on circular machines, gained favour. At the same time dark or coloured stockings, in wide mesh of various textures, seen since 1958 (Fig. 13), were all the vogue (1962–63). Waist-to-toe stretch-nylon tights in royal blue, scarlet, or black were on sale for women and children from *c* 1959, for winter sports and leisure wear.

Long ropes of beads and semi-precious stones (Fig. 4), or elaborate 'bib' necklaces, worn close round the throat (Figs. 12, 17), replaced the once popular pearl necklace.

Floral prints dominated at first in gay, light colours. Delicate pastel shades returned in 1959–63: dusty pinks and lilac, smoky blue, beige and soft tan, also charcoal grey. Mossy, olive, and bronze greens, also coffee, for the winters of 1958 and 1959, when bronze brown replaced black for evening wear, with very dark peat brown in 1960–62. Black returned with white and neutral greys for suits and tweeds, also green with tan, in 1961. Small prints with dark grounds, coin-sized spot patterns, and dark, muted and striped cottons from India were seen in 1961; a bright orange for the young in 1960, with shocking pink in 1961–63. Paisley patterns appeared then, close-toned or brilliant; also rich reds, greens, amber, and greys. Colours were subtle or crisp; for evenings they were rich or subdued, with glitter fabrics from 1961 and black again from 1962.

ELIZABETH II (1952-   )

Women's Fashions: PART III (1963-68)

SKIRTS were short or very short; in 1966 they still continued to go up and up. 'Swinging London' began the mini-skirt fashion, and with its 'way-out' gear it set the pace on both sides of the Atlantic; by 1967 nearly all women who could wore minis. The straight hanging shift replaced the fitting sheath, and 'see-through' dresses with the 'nothing-underneath' look were fashionable from 1965 with stretch suspender-less stockings or panti-hose. Legs were the focus of fashion, with bust, waist, and hips almost ignored. 'Fun' fur coats, 'trendy' prints, violent colours, leather coats and dresses, and the 'maxi look' appeared. Hair was long and straight, or, as a contrast, short and boyish. Trouser suits were 'in', and at times it was difficult to distinguish between the sexes, something that had never occurred before.

The most typical dress of this period was the high-necked straight shift (Fig. 6), with or without sleeves or belt; many older women preferred a slim-line shaped style (Fig. 1), with a matching coat or jacket, it made a dateless two-piece fashionable season after season, being suitable for lunch date, theatre, or cocktail party. The shift could be made in any material from silk to tweed, from Paisley print to metallic sheen glitter for evenings (Fig. 6). It was not unlike the popular sweater dress which could be horizontally striped (Fig. 5), or of Italian 'see through' chunky-knit or crochet from 1965. The pinafore dress was as popular as the leather outfit (Fig. 12), which, when worn with sweater and matching tights, gave the appearance of an outer accessory, with an all-in-one garment underneath. Another fashionable dress from 1966 flared out 'tent-wise', from neckline to hem (Fig. 15), long-sleeved or sleeveless, vertically striped, plain or richly patterned; it was most fashionable made in transparent nylon chiffon, worn over a plain or contrasting sewn-in slip; for evening wear it could be worn long or short, loose, or, from 1968, belted at the waist with a wide, richly decorative band. Most dresses were short above the knee by 1964, with teen-agers usually having the hemline at mid-thigh (Fig. 12). The accent was on youth (Fig. 4), presenting fashion problems for the mature woman. Frilled decoration above the hem on some day dresses (1964-66), or perhaps ostrich feathers on the short evening shift, gave an 'upward' look.

By 1966, the year of the mini skirt, hemlines in London reached seven inches above the knee, and in New York four to five inches. Apart from a very brief lengthening in late 1966, when some maxi skirts appeared (Figs. 8, 16), hemlines went on rising, and by late 1967 many very short styles were seen on the young (Plate VIII), particularly for party wear (Fig. 14).

With the 'see-through' look, lace returned to favour, for short or long slender formal evening dress; also delicate chiffon, hanging straight and slim from shoulder to ankle, was sometimes fully embroidered in beads and sequins, giving an open, lace-like quality, or more often some high-waisted evening gowns had only the tiny bodice or bolero

Marginal notes:
Dress
Shift
Two-piece

Sweater
dress
See-through
Pinafore
dress
*Tent-dress,
short
or long*

Mini skirt

Maxi skirt

Beaded

top so decorated. Other evening tops, which could be worn with a mini skirt, were of open-mesh knit-embroidered in pearls, beads, or sequins (Fig. 14).

By 1967 some day dresses had a flared skirt, and in 1968 this line was well established, usually with a slightly lowered hemline and long, slender look to the waist (Fig. 17). Necklines generally remained high.

Paper dresses   Disposable paper dresses were launched in the autumn of 1967, some of paper with nylon, others of paper with non-woven cellulose material; the short, straight style was fairly successful, but at this early stage they were insufficiently crease-resistant or fire-proof. As overalls or disposable underwear for holiday use the material had obvious value.

Culottes   From 1965 the culotte dress in silk or nylon mixtures (Fig. 11), in op-art designs of black and white or violently contrasting colours, was seen increasingly for evening wear or parties. The 'trousers' were often extremely wide, giving the appearance of a very full skirt. By 1967 some were short or of mid-thigh length for day wear.

Caftan   A long, robe-like garment, the caftan, appeared in 1967 for evening relaxation; it hung straight and unbelted, as worn in the Middle East, slightly flaring from neck to ankle, with long sleeves. It could be made in softly patterned wools or rich furnishing fabrics.

Sleeves   Long sleeves now reached to the wrist, fitting (Fig. 17), flared (Fig. 5), or with plain or with frilled cuffs (Fig. 16). The popular sleeveless style was often cut well back, leaving the shoulder bare (Figs. 11, 15).

Skirts   Short, slim, straight skirts, usually fully lined, were in a wide range of materials from tweeds and leather (Figs. 2, 12, Plate VIII) to the popular crease-resistant, non-stretch jersey fabrics (Fig. 14). In 1965–67 a gored or pleated tartan skirt (Fig. 4) was made with matching stretch-nylon tights or sweater; or of a tweed, with sweater and tights matching, making the skirt to appear an outer accessory. From 1966 full-length slim skirts in tweeds, Scottish tartans, or other fabrics such as velvet were most fashionable for formal evening wear or cocktail parties (Fig. 16), especially the tartans.

Knitwear   Well-styled knitwear, cardigan or sweater, was still a most useful item for leisure wear (Fig. 4), in finest wools to Bri-nylon, chunky knits to open, lace-like textures. Thick, richly patterned Aran sweaters were popular from 1966.

Trouser suit   Paris introduced the trouser suit in 1964 as a fashionable outfit, not just for sport or holiday use, but for town, country, house, or evening wear; it was universally adopted, particularly in England, and was worn by all age groups. With a straight or tailored jacket (Figs. 3, 13), it was made in tweeds or corduroys, cream twill for summer or Lurex jersey for evenings; some smart London hotels, though, would not accept such unconventional attire.

Tabard   In 1965 a sleeveless, hip-length jacket or tabard, identical back and front, and fastening on the shoulders, was popular, particularly in zebra-printed kid over a polo-necked jersey, worn with straight or sometimes bell-bottomed trousers in 1964–67.

Jeans   Anoraks and jeans, previously confined to holiday wear, were increasingly used for casual winter wear in town or country, by children, teen-agers, men, and women.

Coat   From 1964 the reversible coat was one of the most popular (Fig. 1), usually of plain tweed, reversing to plaid, with a matching dress or two-piece suit. It could reverse dark with a light colour or stripe with plain; it could be made in a proofed poplin, reversing to wool and camel-hair cloth. For travel or week-end wear it was ideal. Coats

190

Elizabeth II (1952–)
part III (1963-68)

1

2

3

4

5

6

7

8

9

10

from 1964

'66 -'67

'64 -'67

'65

'66

from '65

'66 -'68

'67 -'68

11

12

13

14

15

16

17

from 1965

from 1964

from 1964

1967-'68

'66 -'68

from 1966

1968

were almost any length, full or three-quarter (Figs. 1, 2), or short and straight (Fig. 3), when they could be worn with slim skirt or trousers. The mini coat from 1965 was most fashionable in natural or coloured leathers (Fig. 7); it was straight with little shaping, as were most other coats. But from 1967 the flared suède coat (Fig. 10), belted or plain, and often lined with an Orlon pile fabric, was extremely popular. Cloth and tweed coats were also made in these styles. The long, flared maxi coat introduced in 1966 (Fig. 8) was normal- or high-waisted, plain or belted, but it was not generally adopted.

By 1967 capes, tailored to fit the shoulders and hanging full but straight, were being worn by many young women, of tweed or often proofed tartan; some were made with matching deerstalker hats.

Many low- and medium-priced 'pop' coats and jackets in gaily dyed rabbit skins were fancied by teen-agers from 1965. More expensive, long-haired furs, worked horizontally, were highly fashionable for jackets or coats from 1966 (Fig. 9); these were sometimes worn belted in 1967–68. Shorter-haired furs such as kid, calf, pony-skin, lamb, leopard, and tiger, were also used for coats and jackets, as well as fur pile fabrics of Acrilan or Orlon.

Shiny PVC coats continued; also a new thin 'wet-look' nylon was used. Most fabrics by 1961 could be made water-repellent with a silicone finish; thus a Terylene voile dress could have its own matching shower-proof coat. In 1962–63 iridescent shower-proof poplins were new for rain-wear.

Jersey, made in wool, cotton, silk, rayon, synthetic fibres, and a wide range of mixtures, continued as the most wearable fabric on the market. In 1968 a new bonded jersey had the lining incorporated in the cloth, making it hang and keep its shape even better than before. In 1966 there was a new printed jersey in Crimplene, made soft and smooth or crisp and chunky; it was another fabric which increased rapidly in popularity by 1968, as it was remarkable for keeping its shape and its easy-care qualities. Tweeds were used for day or evening wear, and leather and suède were highly fashionable, even for dresses in 1968. Contrasting with this, from 1965, lace and fabrics with a 'see-through' mesh were popular, and delicate, transparent materials such as gossamer wool chiffon, silk or nylon chiffon, Terylene lawn and voiles, and very lightweight, totally uncrushable Bri-nylons were seen everywhere for summer and evenings; they were ideal for travelling, being light and crease-resistant and taking up little space. Crêpes became fashionable, with a new cotton-crêpe in 1966, a soft, warm fabric, a new Tricel-and-wool crêpe in 1968, also a moss crêpe. By 1966 evening and many summer dresses were romantic and flowery, with printed chiffons, silks, crêpes, shantung, and satin, also cloqués and velvet.

From 1964 preformed bra-cups were used in swim-suits and beach wear, also in slips; later, by 1968, they were used in day or evening dresses.

With the 'nothing-underneath' look, a body stocking, similar to a flesh-coloured stretch swim-suit, was produced in October 1964, but in 1965 an improved controlling foundation was made of flesh-coloured Lycra Spandex, giving 'lift', as well as veiling the form.

Zip fasteners, with a large pendant ring, were often used in 1964–65 as a decorative front fastening (Fig. 12); otherwise dresses were zip-fastened at the back.

Long, shining hair now went with the 'swinging' styles (Figs. 11, 12, and Plate VIII). For special occasions it was often aided by wigs or switches (Fig. 14). Some teen-agers wore this long hair covering one eye, a fashion also seen in some of the short

192

styles in 1965–66 (Fig. 15). Back combing and the use of lacquer fixatives were now deplored. Fringes were popular with long or various short hair styles, or the hair was drawn back off the face (Figs. 10, 14, 17). A mop of thick rolled curls was sometimes seen from 1966 with the maxi skirt (Fig. 8). In 1967–68 a piled-up, frizzed mop was affected by some hippies and teen-agers. Heavy eye make-up continued, and lips were pale; iridescent lipstick and nail varnish were used in the mid-sixties; tinted spectacles were fancied. Make-up
Tinted
spectacles

Various tall-crowned hats with wide or narrow brims (Fig. 1) were most fashionable, also the upturned Breton styles (Fig. 2). 'Costermonger' caps were worn, matching the leather or PVC coats (Fig. 7), and fur hats were popular for winter wear (Figs. 8, 9). Hats

The chisel toe with set-back heel and straps of 1965 (Figs. 4, 15) was followed by sling-backs on even heavier models (Fig. 17), with most shoes having square toes, chunky set-back heels (Figs. 14, 16), often with tongues or the highly fashionable buckle (Figs. 5, 11, Plate VIII). From 1965 bi-colour treatments or two different materials were used, also patent leathers in a wide range of colours. By late 1965 a new synthetic material was tested, and by 1968 was being used for many women's and some men's shoes, besides the usual leather. It was a poromeric material called 'Corfam', using urethane polymer material with polyester reinforcement. It was cool and comfortable to wear, kept its shape and appearance, and was cleaned with a damp rag. Shoes

*Poromeric
material*

Fitting suède and leather boots were now high fashion, reaching sometimes to above the knee; they were extremely popular, especially with the mini skirt (Figs. 7, 9, 10, 12). Mid-calf white kid boots appeared in 1965. Boots

Seam-free stockings continued, but longer, suspenderless ones called 'hold-ups' were produced in Germany in 1965 and in England in 1967. Flesh-coloured, seamless stockings from waist to toe, first made on circular machines in 1962 and called panti-hose, were selling in the shops by 1966 (Figs. 14, 15, 17, Plate VIII), becoming by 1968 a staple requirement in most young and many older women's wardrobes. Coloured tights, previously worn for sport or leisure wear, were by 1965 made in a wide variety of patterns and colours for everyday use (Figs. 4, 6); also white, black, or coloured stockings in open-mesh, coarse-knit, or lace-like textures were popular in 1964–66 (Fig. 12). Gaily coloured or patterned socks (Fig. 5) were also popular from 1964 to 1966. Stockings
Hold-ups
Panti-hose

Socks

Large, chunky op-art jewellery with rings and bracelets (Figs. 11, 12), rows of chains and beads, were fancied by teen-agers in 1965, with large hooped earrings in cheaper ranges in 1966 (Fig. 6). In 1967 fine-quality Indian yoke necklaces and bracelets were fashionable (Fig. 15). Jewellery

Piercing, vivid off-beat colours with Oriental flower designs and giant floral prints which appeared in 1963 continued, with op-art designs and large or small Paisley patterns being particularly popular. Bright and glowing striped patterns, horizontal or vertical, were seen in 1966 and 1967, a larger version of the 1961 stripes. Some tartans and checks were brilliant; also off-beat colours were seen in tweeds, grape and amber, charcoal and biscuit, or yellow, hot orange, and lime. Eye-dazzling vivid prints in psychedelic colours had a brief life in 1967. By 1968 colours and patterns were more subtle, with white, black, cool greys, and rich autumn shades being popular, with many soft pastel colours and beiges. Tones also were discreet in 1964. Glitter fabrics with silver trimmings and accessories were in favour in 1966. Irish and Scottish tweeds, hand- or machine-woven, were made in superb ranges of colours, weights, and textures. Colours

193

FURTHER READING

ADBURGHAM, ALISON: *A Punch History of Manners and Modes, 1841–1940* (1961).

BOEHN, MAX VON: *Modes and Manners*, vols. i, ii, iii, iv, v, vi (1932, etc.).

BOTT, ALAN: *Our Fathers, 1870–1900* (1931).

BOTT, ALAN, AND IRENE CLEPHANE: *Our Mothers, 1870–1900* (1932).

BUCK, ANNE: *Victorian Costume and Costume Accessories* (1961).

CALTHROP, D. C.: *English Costume, 1066–1830* (1923).

CROSSLEY, FRED: *English Church Monuments* (1921).

CUNNINGTON, C. W.: *Englishwomen's Clothing in the Nineteenth Century* (1937).

———— *Englishwomen's Clothing in the Present Century* (1952).

———— *The Art of English Costume* (1948).

CUNNINGTON, C. W. AND P., AND CHARLES BEARD: *A Dictionary of English Costume* (1960).

CUNNINGTON, C. W. AND P.: *Handbooks of English Costume in the Sixteenth, Seventeenth, Eighteenth, and Nineteenth Centuries* (1962–64, 1959).

CUNNINGTON, P., AND ANNE BUCK: *Children's Costume in England, 1300–1900* (1965).

ESDAILE, ARUNDELL, Mrs: *English Church Monuments, 1510–1840* (1946).

FRYER, ALFRED: *Wooden Monumental Effigies in England and Wales* (1924).

GAIRDNER, JAMES (editor): *The Paston Letters, 1422–1509* (1901).

GERNSHEIM, ALISON: *Fashion and Reality, 1840–1914* (1963).

GIBBS-SMITH, CHARLES: *The Fashionable Lady in the Nineteenth Century* (1960).

HARTLEY, D., AND M. M. ELLIOT: *Life and Work of the People of England*, vols. i and ii, 1000–1500 and 1500–1800 (1925).

HOLLAND, VYVYAN: Handcoloured Fashion Plates, 1770–1899 (1955).

KELLY, F. M., AND RANDOLPH SCHWABE: *Historic Costume, 1490–1790* (1925).

KÖHLER, CARL: *A History of Costume* (1928).

LAVER, JAMES: *Early Tudor, 1485–1558* (1951), Costume of the Western World Series.

———— *Taste and Fashion, from the French Revolution to the Present Day* (1945).

LINTHICUM, M. C.: *Costume in the Drama of Shakespeare and his Contemporaries* (1936).

MACKLIN, H. W.: *The Brasses of England* (1904).

PEPYS, SAMUEL: *Diary and Correspondence, deciphered by the Rev. J. Smith* (1898).

PLANCHÉ, J. R.: *British Costume* (1874).

———— *Cyclopædia of Costume* (1876–79).

REYNOLDS, GRAHAM: *Elizabethan and Jacobean, 1558–1625* (1951), Costume of the Western World Series.

Royal Commission on Historic Monuments in London, vol. i, *Westminster Abbey*.

SALZMANN, L. F.: *English Life in the Middle Ages* (1926).

———— *England in Tudor Times* (1926).

THOMSON, HELEN: *Fibres and Fabrics of Today* (1967).
WAUGH, NORAH: *Corsets and Crinolines* (1954).

MUSEUMS

London Museum: Catalogue No. 5, *Costume.*
Manchester City Art Galleries: *Gallery of English Costume,* booklets i–vii.
Victoria and Albert Museum: *Brass Rubbings,* illustrated catalogue.
————— *Seventeenth- and Eighteenth-century Costume* (1959).
————— *Nineteenth-century Costume.*

PERIODICALS AND PAPERS

La Belle Assemblée, 1806–9, 1817–30.
The Englishwoman's Domestic Magazine.
Le Journal des Demoiselles.
The Ladies' Cabinet.
The Ladies' Field.
The Lady's Magazine.
Britannica Book of the-Year, 1937–56 and 1956–68.
Country Life, 1897–1916 and 1922–68.
The Illustrated London News, 1847–1913 and 1918–68.
Picture Post.
Punch, 1841–1900 and 1903–68.
The Sphere.
Sunday Times.
Time Magazine.

The Ladies' Treasury.
The Lady's Monthly Museum.
The Lady's Own Paper.
The Queen.
Silvia's Home Journal.

Daily Telegraph and Morning Post.
Manchester Guardian.
The Observer.

INDEX

The abbreviations (m.) pp. *and* (f.) pp. *signify respectively 'men's pages only' and 'women's pages only'.*